Learning for Earning

Your Route to Success

Teacher's Annotated Workbook

by

John A. Wanat
Consultant and Author on Occupational Education
Jackson, New Jersey

E. Weston Pfeiffer
Consultant on Technical and Vocational Training
Lambertville, New Jersey

Richard Van Gulik, PhD
Assistant Director—Curriculum
Withlacoochee Technical Institute
Inverness, Florida

Publisher
The Goodheart-Willcox Company, Inc.
Tinley Park, Illinois
www.g-w.com

Introduction

This *Student Workbook* is designed for use with the text *Learning for Earning: Your Route to Success*. It will help you understand and remember the facts and concepts about career exploration presented in the text. It will also help you apply what you learn to your everyday life.

The activities in this workbook are divided into chapters that correspond to those in the text. By reading the text first, you will have the information needed to complete the activities. Try to complete them without referring to the text. Later, you can check the text to complete any answer you did not finish. At that time, you can also compare your answers to the information in the text.

Most of the *Workbook's* activities are designed to stimulate your thinking and help you apply the new information. These ask for your opinions and ideas, so there are no right or wrong answers. Other activities have right answers and can be used as review guides when you study for tests and quizzes. An example is the vocabulary exercise that begins each chapter. It uses a matching or fill-in-the-blank activity or a crossword puzzle to review the new terms introduced in the text.

Exploring careers is fun but, more importantly, it opens your eyes to the wide range of jobs in the workplace. *Learning for Earning* will help you identify the career that is best for you.

Contents

Part Four — Acquiring Workplace Skills

Part Seven — Growing Toward Independence

The Importance of Work

Reinforcing Vocabulary

Activity A

Chapter 1

Name _____

Date _____ Period _____

Match the following terms with their definitions.

N	1. An activity done to produce or accomplish something.	A. career
G	2. The work a person does, usually to earn money.	B. career clusters
J	3. Employment that requires related skills and experiences.	C. career ladder
A	4. A series of occupations, usually in the same or related fields, that helps you advance in a chosen field of work.	D. economy
		E. identity
C	5. An illustration that shows a sequence of work in a career field, from entry to advanced levels.	F. income
		G. job
F	6. The amount of money a person receives for doing a job.	H. lifestyle
I	7. The basics a person must have in order to live.	I. needs
M	8. The items a person would like to have, but are not needed to survive.	J. occupation
		K. self-esteem
E	9. The sum of traits that distinguishes a person as an individual.	L. transferable skills
		M. wants
H	10. A person's typical way of life.	N. work
K	11. The confidence a person has in himself or herself.	
D	12. The way goods and services are produced, distributed, and consumed in a society.	
B	13. The 16 broad groups of occupational and career specialties.	
L	14. Skills used in one career that can be used in another.	

Your Thoughts on Work

Activity B   **Name** _____

Chapter 1   **Date** _____ **Period** _____

Begin thinking about how your work will fit into your life. Do so by providing answers to the following questions. Then discuss your ideas in class.

1. You will probably have a job because you need income to live. List three other important reasons you will work.

    A. (Sample response.) to use my education _____

    B. (Sample response.) to make a difference in society _____

    C. (Sample response.) to provide satisfaction in life _____

2. List three benefits you hope to gain from working.

    A. (Sample response.) comfortable lifestyle _____

    B. (Sample response.) professional development _____

    C. (Sample response.) to have a feeling of accomplishment _____

3. List five transferable skills you think are important to job success in any type of job.

    A. (Sample response.) artistic skills _____

    B. (Sample response.) critical thinking skills _____

    C. (Sample response.) speaking a second language _____

    D. (Sample response.) computer skills _____

    E. (Sample response.) academic skills _____

4. What type of work interests you? Why? (Student response.) _____

   _____

   _____

   _____

   _____

   _____

   _____

5. What personal qualities would help you succeed in the type of work that interests you? _____

   (Student response.) _____

   _____

   _____

   _____

6. How would doing this type of work affect your lifestyle? (Student response.) _____

   _____

   _____

   _____

Working to Help Others

Activity C

Chapter 1

Name _____

Date _____ Period _____

Throughout history, many people have chosen to do work that helps others. These people are often successful without making a lot of money. Success comes to them in the form of pride and satisfaction in helping others. Answer the following questions about people who work to help society.

1. Name three famous people, living or dead, who have contributed to others while living a simple lifestyle. Include a short statement of each person's accomplishments.

    A. (Sample response.) Helen Keller: taught the world to respect people who are blind or deaf.

    B. (Sample response.) George Washington Carver: an innovator of agricultural science.

    C. (Sample response.) Mother Teresa: a humanitarian and advocate for the poor and helpless.

2. Name three people you know personally who have contributed to others while living a simple lifestyle. Write a short statement of what each person has done.

    A. (Student response.)

    B. (Student response.)

    C. (Student response.)

3. If you were given the chance to talk to any interesting person who works to help others, whom would you choose? Why? (Student response.)

4. List three qualities that most people who help others have in common.

    A. (Sample response.) compassion

    B. (Sample response.) empathy

    C. (Sample response.) consideration

5. What would you like to contribute to society during your own life?

    (Student response.)

Careers That Meet Your Goals

Activity D

Chapter 1

Name _____

Date _____ Period _____

Whether you reach many of your goals in life will depend on the career you choose. List some of your goals related to each topic in the chart. Then list careers that you think would help you meet your goals.

(Student response.)	Your Goals	Careers to Help You Meet Your Goals
1. Income		
2. Identity		
3. Lifestyle		
4. Satisfaction		

Chapter 2
The Changing Workplace

Reinforcing Vocabulary

Activity A   Name _____

Chapter 2   Date _____ Period _____

Match the following terms with their correct definitions.

_H_ 1. An economy in which individuals and businesses play a major role in making decisions.

_M_ 2. The money left in a business after all expenses are paid.

_I_ 3. Goods and services created by companies in one country are sold to customers in other countries.

_O_ 4. Nonmaterial assistance for which people are willing to pay.

_F_ 5. Work programs that help employees to balance the demand of work and family.

_G_ 6. A work schedule that permits flexibility in work hours.

_N_ 7. Individuals who can take care of themselves; who can earn a salary that will support their needs and wants as well as those of their future families.

_B_ 8. The characteristics or makeup of a population.

_C_ 9. The positive result of people of different racial, ethnic, and cultural backgrounds working together.

_L_ 10. The practice of one company contracting with another to handle work more efficiently and keep costs in line.

_P_ 11. The application of scientific principles.

_A_ 12. The total change in the way people live and work caused by computers.

_Q_ 13. Working at home through an electronic linkup with the central office.

_J_ 14. The global computer linkup of individuals, groups, and organizations in government, business, and education.

_E_ 15. Electronic retailing.

_D_ 16. Electronic commerce.

_K_ 17. Continually updating your knowledge and skills.

A. computer revolution
B. demographics
C. diversity
D. e-commerce
E. e-tailing
F. family-friendly programs
G. flextime
H. free enterprise system
I. global economy
J. Internet
K. lifelong learning
L. outsourcing
M. profit
N. self-sufficient
O. services
P. technology
Q. telecommuting

Workplace Solutions

Activity B   **Name** _____

Chapter 2   **Date** _____ **Period** _____

Read the case study below and provide your solutions to the problems of Specialty Products Company.

Case Study

Specialty Products Company has hired you as a consultant. Their earnings have been decreasing in recent years. Your task is to provide the company management with recommendations to help turn the company around and become profitable again.

After six months of study, you have observed the following:

- Specialty Products Company has a high turnover rate among their employees, especially those who are young parents.
- Specialty Products Company only sells their products in the U.S.
- The methods and equipment that Specialty Products Company uses are the same as when they started their business in 1968.
- They spend a large part of their revenues on property landscaping and maintenance.
- The company's employees feel that management doesn't care about their ideas, many of which they feel could help the company operate more efficiently.

List below the recommendations you have for the management of Specialty Products Company. Give reasons for each of your recommendations.

- **Recommendation:** Specialty Product Company should establish an on-site child care center.

  Reason: This could be seen as a valuable benefit to young parents and would help to retain those who are young parents who have difficulty in finding reliable child care.

- **Recommendation:** Specialty Products Company should market their products in other countries.

  Reason: This could help increase company profits.

- **Recommendation:** Specialty Products Company should consider upgrading their methods and equipment with newer technology.

  Reason: This could help the company become more efficient and profitable.

- **Recommendation:** Specialty Products Company should revise their budget to include less money spent on landscaping and maintenance and accept bids from several sources.

  Reason: By trimming the landscaping and maintenance budget, the company can invest in more technology to make the company more efficient and profitable.

- **Recommendation:** Specialty Products Company should welcome employee suggestions and reward employees who find or develop ways to help the company operate more efficiently.

  Reason: This will increase employee morale and make them feel more a part of the team.

Workforce Changes

Activity C   Name _____

Chapter 2   Date _____ Period _____

Many factors are affecting the workforce today and will be in the future. Some of these are listed below. In the space provided, write your ideas of how the changes indicated might impact you and your career decisions.

Workplace Changes	How These Changes Might Impact Me and My Career Decisions
Social Change	I will find a career that will allow me to be self-sufficient.
Population Shifts	I will look for a position with a company with a diverse labor force.
The Economy	A good economy could positively affect my career, while a downturn in the economy could have a negative effect.
World Events	World events can hold opportunities and consequences for my career.
Government Actions	I will stay alert to government plans that may affect my career.
The Forces of Competition on Staff Size	I will look for a position with a company that foresees a long-term demand for its products.

The Computer Revolution

Activity D   Name _____

Chapter 2   Date _____ Period _____

Computers have revolutionized the world of work. Briefly describe or give an example of how each form of technology listed below has affected the way people work.

Invention	How It Affects People Who Work
PC	The PC has brought enormous computing power, resulting in automating the office and combining systems that formerly were kept separate. Now the work of storing, processing, and communicating information has merged into a single system. This allows several computer users to communicate with each other.
Laptops	Laptops have freed people from their desks. Workers can take them to the factory, a meeting room, or a project area, and back to their desks. This also allows more work to be done at home.
Telecommuting	More work can be done at home by sending information back and forth with an electronic linkup with the central office.
Internet	With the right equipment and connections, workers in different locations can share voice or voice/picture communications anytime and anywhere.
E-tailing	Consumers and businesses can sell and buy goods and services over the Internet.
E-commerce	Consumers and businesses can sell and buy goods and services over the Internet.
Fiber-optics	Digital information can be transmitted over long distances. They are also used in medical imaging, mechanical engineering inspection, and for cable television.
Global Positioning System (GPS)	This uses a series of satellites to identify the user's location and is used extensively in the shipping and transportation industries.

The Law in the Workplace

Reinforcing Vocabulary

Activity A

Chapter 3

Name _____

Date _____ Period _____

In this chapter you learned about five government acts that were passed to protect workers' rights. These are listed below. Examples of discrimination relating to the workplace are also described. In the blank spaces below, write the letter of the act that addresses each action. Acts can be used more than once.

A. Age Discrimination Act
B. Americans with Disabilities Act
C. Equal Employment Opportunity Act
D. Equal Pay Act
E. Family and Medical Leave Act

___E___ 1. Mark and Janis had waited many years to adopt a baby. Janis worked for a large ad agency. She was upset when her employer told her she couldn't have any time off from work to be with their new baby.

___B___ 2. Jerome was surprised to see the following question on the job application: Do you have any disabilities?

___C___ 3. Marisa and Jane were both up for a promotion. Both were equally qualified, but Jane got the job. Marisa felt that her race might have had something to do with the decision.

___A___ 4. Ida had raised her children to adulthood. This past year, her husband of 30 years died. She decided to get a job, but the first place she applied turned her down. She was told that she was too old to learn to use a computer.

___D___ 5. Maria discovered that Ben was being paid more for doing the very same job in their office even though they were hired at the same time.

___A___ 6. Mr. Yung had worked 30 years for the Atlas Company when it was bought by another company. The new owners decided to cut payroll costs by letting the oldest employees go.

___C___ 7. Caleb was told that the company had given the job to another applicant. He wondered if it was because he was Jewish.

___E___ 8. Hector's father became gravely ill. He lived with Hector. Without Hector to care for him, he would have to be hospitalized. Hector asked his boss at the large manufacturing plant where he worked if he could take some time off to care for his father in the few weeks he had left to live. His boss turned him down.

___A___ 9. Sheniqua had worked hard to get her college degree, but she looked very young. At the first place she applied, the manager said she was too young to be traveling and making sales calls on her own.

___C___ 10. When Bonnie applied to work at ABC Auto Repair, the owner told her that he didn't hire women to work on cars. It was a man's job.

A Case of Discrimination

Activity B   Name _____

Chapter 3   Date _____ Period _____

Read each of the cases described below and decide if discrimination might have occurred. Record your answers and solutions in the spaces provided.

Case I

Frank was promoted to the position of cashier. He worked in an entry position for 90 days before the promotion. Susan worked for the company full time for almost 18 months and is working as an assistant cashier. Susan believes she was discriminated against by their supervisor. She feels the promotion to the position of cashier should have been hers.

1. Do you think Susan has been discriminated against? _maybe_____

2. What reasons might the employer have for promoting Frank rather than Susan? _____

   _(Sample responses.) Frank might have had more training; Frank might have worked at another_____

   _job as a cashier; Frank might be faster; Frank might make fewer mistakes._____

3. What would you tell Susan to do in this situation? _Susan should speak to her supervisor and find_____

   _out why Frank was promoted over her. The reasons given will determine if Susan has a_____

   _legitimate complaint._____

4. What reason would Susan have for filing a discrimination complaint? _If the only difference between_____

   Susan and Frank is the length of employment, then she might have a legitimate discrimination case.

Case II

Mr. Rojaz was recently laid off from his job. He had worked for the company for 17 years. During that time, he had received five promotions, and he thought he was due for another one. Mr. Rojaz said he should have suspected the layoff because the company favors giving younger employees a chance. Most of his coworkers were also dismissed when they were about his age.

1. Do you think Mr. Rojaz has been discriminated against? _maybe_____

2. What reasons might the employer have for letting Mr. Rojaz go? _(Sample responses.) His work was_____

   _not what it had been; the company was losing money and had to cut back jobs._____

3. What would you tell Mr. Rojaz to do in this situation? _Mr. Rojaz should begin by speaking to his_____

   _supervisor. If he is a member of a union, he could speak to his union representative. If he is not_____

   _given a good reason for his dismissal, he might want to speak with someone from the EEOC._____

4. What reasons would Mr. Rojaz have for a discrimination complaint? _If it can be determined that_____

   _Mr. Rojaz was still a good worker, but was laid off because the company wanted to reduce salaries_____

   _paid to long-term employees, then he might have a legitimate discrimination case._____

Is This Sexual Harassment?

Activity C

Chapter 3

Name _____

Date _____ Period _____

Read each of the statements given below. Decide whether the situation describes possible sexual harassment. Give the reasons for your conclusions.

1. "We have always had men and women working here. They always worked well together. We've always told jokes to each other. What's the big deal? Now that someone new is here, we can't tell jokes anymore?"

   Yes, if the jokes are offensive to the new employee. Jokes can be told in private to people who

   are not offended by them. If a fellow worker indicates that the jokes are offensive, then the person

   telling the jokes should stop telling them. If the jokes continue, then there could be a case for

   sexual harassment.

2. "Look, this is a body shop. Our suppliers provide us with the calendars. So some of them have naked models. So what? Is that a crime?"

   Yes. A hostile environment includes offensive calendars.

3. "I was not talking to them. That conversation was between the two of us. How can that be harassment?"

   This is probably not sexual harassment, but employees need to be considerate of other employees,

   especially if privacy is not possible at work and conversations are easily overheard. Such

   conversations should be saved for after-hours. If an employee is told to do this, and he or she does

   not, then it could possibly be sexual harassment.

4. "This has always been all women employees in this part of the company. He's a guy. How can we be sexually harassing him?"

   It is possible that the women are verbally or nonverbally harassing this man. Not enough

   information is given.

5. "I don't like Mr. Jones. He's always on my case. I'm going to charge him with sexual harassment. That will fix him. Besides, what can happen to me?"

   It is illegal to charge someone with a crime they did not commit—even sexual harassment.

Taking Action

Activity D
Chapter 3

Name _____

Date _____ Period _____

Read the case study below. Then answer the questions that follow.

Case Study

Marsha began working for QTY Construction Company right after she graduated from high school. After attending an apprentice orientation meeting, she was sent to a construction site and assigned to a journey worker. The journey worker was to be her trainer for the first 1000 hours of the apprenticeship. When Marsha arrived at the job site, some of the journey workers began to kid her about being the only woman on the job. She was embarrassed by some of their comments, and she told them to stop. Several weeks passed and the comments continued. Then someone began leaving notes on her car.

Marsha told her trainer what was happening. He responded, "They give all the new apprentices the business. They just want to see if you can take it. I suggest you forget it if you want to complete this program. They're not doing anything different to you than to any other new worker. They were told to treat you just like one of the guys."

1. Do you think any law is being broken at this worksite? If so, what law? Give reasons for your answer.
   Yes; the Civil Rights Act. Reasons: There are indications of a hostile environment, including being kidded, being embarrassed by comments, and having notes left on her car. She asked her fellow workers to stop their behavior, and they did not. She also asked her trainer to intervene and he did nothing. He also threatened her with the completion of the program if she didn't go along with the treatment.

2. What action should Marsha take at this point? She should send a letter to her journey worker and other workers involved telling them to stop and the reason why. She should keep copies of her letters. She should write down all the important details of the events as soon as they occur, including names of people who can support her claim. She should then go to someone higher in the company. There may be a person designated by the company to handle such complaints. Finally, she can contact the EEOC.

Chapter 4
Learning About Careers

Reinforcing Vocabulary

Activity A   **Name** _____

Chapter 4   **Date** _____ **Period** _____

Use each of the terms or phrases listed below in a sentence that shows you understand the meaning of the term or phrase. (Sample responses.)

1. *traits*

   Sentence: _Her trait of honesty is valued at the bank where she works._

2. *education*

   Sentence: _A good education will help you to succeed in life and at work._

3. *training*

   Sentence: _Many jobs require specialized training._

4. *skills*

   Sentence: _Good skills help you to do your job well._

5. *entry-level jobs*

   Sentence: _He accepted an entry-level job as soon as he graduated._

6. *advanced training*

   Sentence: _Her new position will require advanced training._

7. *internship*

   Sentence: _He will learn about publishing during his internship at the newspaper._

8. *promotion*

   Sentence: _She worked hard and earned a promotion to a higher level in the company._

9. *fringe benefits*

   Sentence: _The company offered fringe benefits, such as paid vacation time and insurance._

10. *cost of living*

    Sentence: _He found the cost of living to be higher in New York than in Atlanta._

11. *job shadowing*

    Sentence: _Her job shadowing experience allowed her to see what a florist does._

12. *cooperative education*

    Sentence: _Through cooperative education, he took classes and learned on the job._

Investigating Job Factors

Activity B	Name _____
Chapter 4	Date _____ Period _____

Choose a career that is of interest to you. Using various resources described in this chapter, answer the following questions about basic job factors. Then cite the source you used to answer each question.

Career: _Accountant_

1. What are the main duties and responsibilities of this job? _tax preparation; bookkeeping; auditing;_ _billing; posting; analyze business budgets; prepare financial statements; project future revenues_

   Source: _O*NET_

2. What are the job prospects for this career? _Strong growth of accountant is expected to result from_ _stricter accounting and auditing regulations, along with an expanding economy. The best job_ _prospects will be for accountants and auditors who have a college degree or any certification,_ _but especially a CPA._

   Source: _Occupational Outlook Handbook_

3. What education, training, and skills are required for this job? _Education: a college degree in accounting;_ _Many accountants choose to obtain certification to help advance their careers, such as becoming a_ _Certified Public Accountant (CPA). Skills: mathematics, oral and written communication, analytical_ _competencies, teaming and working in diverse groups, interpersonal and critical thinking;_ _advanced training._

   Source: _The Wall Street Journal_

4. What is the typical starting salary for this job? _$43,809 per year_

   Source: _The Wall Street Journal_

5. Is there opportunity for advancement in this career due to rapid growth in the field? Explain your answer.
   Yes. Faster-than-average growth of accountant jobs will result from an increase in the number of _businesses, changing financial laws and regulations, and greater scrutiny of company finances._

   Source: _Occupational Outlook Handbook_

6. Is this job available in most communities in this country? Explain your answer. _____
   Yes. Accountants are needed in most businesses.

   Source: _Guide for Occupational Exploration_

7. Describe the typical work environment for this job. _Most accountants and auditors work in a typical_ _office setting. Some may be able to do part of their work at home._

   Source: _Occupational Outlook Handbook_

Obtaining Career Information

Activity C

Chapter 4

Name _____

Date _____ Period _____

There are many ways to get the facts on jobs that interest you. Many of these ways are given below, but you need to supply the missing letters. Then complete each statement.

1. The <u>O</u> * <u>N</u> <u>E</u> <u>T</u> is a good place to start your career information search because _____
   it can be used to explore careers, related job skills, and trends. It also provides tools for assessing a
   person's abilities and interests. _____

2. The G <u>u</u> <u>i</u> <u>d</u> <u>e</u> for O <u>c</u> <u>c</u> <u>u</u> <u>p</u> <u>a</u> <u>t</u> <u>i</u> <u>o</u> <u>n</u> <u>a</u> <u>l</u> Exploration is designed to help people
   understand what traits are required for certain occupations. _____
   _____
   _____

3. A school C <u>o</u> <u>u</u> <u>n</u> S <u>e</u> <u>l</u> <u>o</u> <u>r</u> can help you find out such information as _____
   careers and their educational requirements, colleges and trade or technical schools offering
   specific programs, government service and recruiting information, and local opportunities to
   observe jobs in your career field. _____

4. If your computer is online, you can use the <u>I</u> N <u>t</u> <u>e</u> <u>r</u> N <u>e</u> <u>t</u> to find out such information as
   details about unions, professional associations, employment agencies, companies, newsgroups
   and electronic message boards. _____

5. Public <u>e</u> <u>m</u> P <u>l</u> <u>o</u> Y <u>m</u> <u>e</u> <u>n</u> <u>t</u> services exist to help people find employment.
   _____

6. By <u>i</u> <u>n</u> T <u>e</u> <u>r</u> <u>v</u> <u>i</u> <u>e</u> W <u>i</u> <u>n</u> <u>g</u> people who work in a field, you can learn _____
   about their jobs and career field. _____
   _____

7. J <u>o</u> <u>b</u> S <u>h</u> <u>a</u> <u>d</u> <u>o</u> <u>w</u> <u>i</u> <u>n</u> <u>g</u> even for a few days is enough time to experience the work
   environment firsthand and get your career questions answered. You also witness the type of duties
   commonly performed. _____

8. By <u>v</u> <u>o</u> <u>l</u> U <u>n</u> T <u>e</u> <u>e</u> <u>r</u> <u>i</u> <u>n</u> <u>g</u> for community organizations you can _____
   gain firsthand experience. _____

9. One of the things you can learn from a <u>p</u> <u>a</u> <u>r</u> <u>t</u>- <u>t</u> I <u>m</u> <u>e</u> job is _____
   following company policies and interacting with fellow workers. _____

10. Schools often have <u>c</u> A <u>r</u> E <u>e</u> <u>r</u> days where they invite employers and other speakers to _____
    give you helpful hints on how to learn more about your particular interests. _____
    _____

Getting to Know Career Information Sources

Activity D   Name _____

Chapter 4   Date _____ Period _____

Visit your school or community library. See how many different types of sources of career information you can find there. You may ask a librarian for assistance. Describe each source below and then copy a sample of career information from each source.   (Sample responses.)

1. Description of source: America's Job Bank _____

   Sample of career information from this source: Includes a nationwide job bank and links _____

   to individual state job banks. _____

   _____

   _____

   _____

2. Description of source: Career Builder _____

   Sample of career information from this source: National and local employment network _____

   plus extensive links to local, regional, and national newspapers. _____

   _____

   _____

   _____

3. Description of source: Monster.com _____

   Sample of career information from this source: A recruiting site containing 50,000 job listings, _____

   databases, employer information and more. Internship opportunities also listed. _____

   _____

   _____

   _____

4. Description of source: College Grad Job Hunt _____

   Sample of career information from this source: Help for finding that first real job, including résumé _____

   development and posting, and interviewing tips. Also links to many job databases. _____

   _____

   _____

   _____

5. Description of source: U.S.JobNet.com _____

   Sample of career information from this source: Full-time or part-time employment listings. Post your _____

   résumé and perform an in-depth job search in a comprehensive job listings database. _____

   _____

   _____

   _____

Chapter 5
Types of Careers

Reinforcing Vocabulary

Activity A

Chapter 5

Name _____

Date _____ Period _____

Match the following career clusters with their descriptions.

__P__ 1. Careers that involve moving people and freight on land, at sea, and in the air.

__C__ 2. Careers that include acting, writing, printing, and producing videos.

__A__ 3. Careers that relate to working with plants, animals, food processing, and the environment.

__J__ 4. Careers that relate to improving a person's quality of life.

__M__ 5. Careers that involve production work in factories.

__D__ 6. Careers that involve clerical, computer, accounting, management, and administrative work.

__B__ 7. Careers that involve building and designing roads, bridges, and buildings.

__F__ 8. Careers that involve the handling of money through banking, investing and accounting.

__G__ 9. Careers that provide legislative, administrative, and regulatory services.

__N__ 10. Careers that involve the promoting, buying, and selling of goods and services.

__L__ 11. Careers that involve judicial, legal, and protective services.

__I__ 12. Careers that involve making visitors happy.

__K__ 13. Careers that involve designing, developing, managing, and supporting hardware and software information systems.

__O__ 14. Careers that involve research as well as laboratory and testing services resulting in discoveries with the potential for improving life.

__H__ 15. Careers that involve promoting health, wellness, and diagnosis as well as treating injuries and diseases.

__E__ 16. Careers that involve training, guidance counseling, coaching, and library services.

A. Agriculture, Food, and Natural Resources

B. Architecture and Construction

C. Arts, Audio/Video Technology, and Communications

D. Business, Management, and Administration

E. Education and Training

F. Finance

G. Government and Public Administration

H. Health Science

I. Hospitality and Tourism

J. Human Services

K. Information Technology

L. Law, Public Safety, Corrections, and Security

M. Manufacturing

N. Marketing, Sales, and Service

O. Science, Technology, Engineering, and Mathematics

P. Transportation, Distribution, and Logistics

Occupational Research

Activity B   Name _____

Chapter 5   Date _____ Period _____

Select one occupation that interests you and answer the following questions about that occupation. Use the sources indicated to acquire information about it. Share the results of your research orally in class. (Sample responses are shown.)

1. What is the title of an occupation that interests you? _automotive technician_____

2. Before consulting a resource, describe what you think people in this occupation do. _____
   _People in this occupation repair cars._____
   _____

3. Consult career publications, Internet sites, videos, and CD-ROMs, and summarize their description of this occupation. _Automotive technicians inspect, repair, and maintain automobiles._____
   _____
   _____
   _____
   _____

4. Where do people in this occupation work? _Generally they work indoors in well-ventilated_____
   _repair shops. However, some shops are drafty and noisy._____
   _____

5. What is the general employment outlook for this occupation in five years? in 10 years? _Employment_
   of automotive service technicians is expected to increase 14 percent between 2006 and 2016.

6. How many people are employed in this occupation? _approximately 783,000_____

7. What local companies employ workers in this occupation? _(Student response.)_____
   _____

8. In the following chart, list the major types of tools, equipment, machines, and materials used by workers in this occupation.

Tools	**Equipment**
handtools such as screwdrivers, pliers, and wrenches, power tools, such as pneumatic wrenches	flame-cutting equipment, jacks, hoists, engine analyzers, alignment equipment
Machines	**Materials**
lathes, grinding machines, wheel balancing machines	lubricants, metals, rubber, refrigerants

(Continued)

Name _____

9. Will you need training beyond high school for this occupation? _____Yes_____ If so, what kind and amount of training will you need?

What Kind of Training?	How Much Training?
_____ On-the-job training _____ Apprenticeship _✔_ Trade or technical school _____ Community college _____ College or university _____ Military	Some trade and technical school programs provide concentrated training for 6 months to a year, depending on how many hours the student attends each week, and award a certificate.

10. List qualifications other than education that are necessary in this occupation.

Physical Qualifications: _Technicians must be able to work in awkward positions. They often lift heavy parts and tools._

Mental Qualifications: _mechanical aptitude, good reasoning ability, diagnostic skills, analytical skills_

Emotional Qualifications: _good communication skills_

11. What are some similar occupations? _automotive body repairers, diesel service technicians, small engine technicians_

12. Is the work dangerous? _It can be dangerous._

 If so, in what way? _Minor cuts, burns, and bruises are common, but technicians can usually avoid serious accidents if safe practices are observed._

 What precautions do workers take to ensure their safety? _Workers must follow accepted safety practices when using tools or machinery and wear protective eyewear, gloves, etc._

13. Is the work seasonal? _No. Work is available year-round._

 If so, when are peak employment periods? _____

 When are the off-seasons? _____

 Are layoffs common during off-seasons? _____

14. Would you have to move from the area to be employed in this occupation? _____
 No. Work is available in all areas.

(Continued)

Name _____

15. Compare your qualifications with the qualifications needed to work in this occupation.
    (Student response.)

My Qualifications	Required Qualifications
_____	_____
_____	_____
_____	_____
_____	_____
_____	_____
_____	_____
_____	_____
_____	_____
_____	_____
_____	_____

16. How can you develop any qualifications you are lacking? (Student response.)
    _____
    _____

17. What have you learned about this occupation through job shadowing, career study tours, guest
    speakers, career fairs, and simulated work activities? (Student response.)
    _____
    _____
    _____
    _____

18. Does this occupation still appeal to you? Explain. (Student response.)
    _____
    _____
    _____
    _____

Exploring Career Clusters

Activity C   Name _____

Chapter 5   Date _____ Period _____

The 16 career clusters described in this chapter are listed below. Place a check in front of the career clusters that interest you. (Sample responses are shown.)

✔ Agriculture, Food, and Natural Resources	✔ Hospitality and Tourism
___ Architecture and Construction	___ Human Services
___ Arts, Audio/Video Technology, and Communications	___ Information Technology
___ Business, Management, and Administration	___ Law, Public Safety, Corrections, and Security
___ Education and Training	___ Manufacturing
✔ Finance	___ Marketing, Sales, and Service
___ Government and Public Administration	___ Science, Technology, Engineering, and Mathematics
___ Health Science	✔ Transportation, Distribution, and Logistics

In the space below, indicate the career clusters you checked and list at least two occupations for each cluster. Explain your interest in each occupation.

Name of cluster: _Agriculture, Food, and Natural Resources_

Occupations:	Reasons for your interest:
1. _Water Quality Manager_	_(Student response.)_
2. _Food Scientist_	_(Student response.)_
3. _____	_____
4. _____	_____

Name of cluster: _Finance_

Occupations:	Reasons for your interest:
1. _Economist_	_(Student response.)_
2. _Insurance Appraiser_	_(Student response.)_
3. _____	_____
4. _____	_____

Name of cluster: _Hospitality and Tourism_

Occupations:	Reasons for your interest:
1. _Caterer_	_(Student response.)_
2. _Travel Agent_	_(Student response.)_
3. _____	_____
4. _____	_____

(Continued)

Name _____

Name of cluster: Transportation, Distribution, and Logistics	
Occupations:	Reasons for your interest:
1. Air Traffic Controller	(Student response.)
2. Cargo and Freight Manager	(Student response.)
3. _____	_____
4. _____	_____

From all the occupations you listed, identify the two that interest you most.

Occupation 1: Air Traffic Controller

Occupation 2: Travel Agent

List the abilities and skills needed for the occupations listed above.

Occupation 1: Must enroll in an FAA-approved education program and pass a pre-employment test that measures the applicant's ability to learn the controller's duties. Must be intelligent, have a good memory, be decisive, have the ability to concentrate, and be articulate to give pilots directions quickly and clearly.

Occupation 2: A love of travel and knowledge and enthusiasm for advising people about travel destinations and itineraries Excellent communication and computer skills are essential for talking with clients and making travel reservations.

Do you have the abilities and skills listed? What can you do to develop any abilities and skills you do not have?

(Student response.)

_____
_____
_____
_____
_____
_____
_____
_____
_____
_____
_____
_____
_____
_____

Chapter 6
A Business of Your Own

Reinforcing Vocabulary

Activity A

Chapter 6

Name _____

Date _____ Period _____

Match the following terms with their correct definitions.

__A__	1. A business that can legally act as a single person, even though many people may own it.	A. corporation
__E__	2. A business that sells products.	B. entrepreneurship
__B__	3. Starting and owning a business of your own.	C. franchise
__G__	4. The easiest type of business to start and dissolve.	D. partnership
__H__	5. Someone who owns a share or shares of a corporation.	E. retail
__C__	6. The right to sell a company's products in a specified area.	F. service
__D__	7. A type of business organization formed when two or more people combine their money and energy.	G. sole proprietorship
__F__	8. A business that performs tasks for customers.	H. stockholder
__J__	9. Money needed to start and maintain a business.	I. wholesale
__I__	10. A large quantity of items packaged in bulk with a per-item cost below the retail price.	J. working capital

Retail and Service Businesses

Activity B Name _____

Chapter 6 Date _____ Period _____

Answer the following questions about retail and service businesses. (Student response.)

1. What kinds of retail businesses do you patronize? _____

2. List five retail businesses in your community and identify the types of products sold by each one.

Business	Products
A. _____	_____
B. _____	_____
C. _____	_____
D. _____	_____
E. _____	_____

3. If you were starting a retail business, what kinds of products would you sell?_____
_____

4. Why would you want to sell these kinds of products? _____
_____

5. Why do you think people would want to buy these kinds of products?_____
_____

6. List three franchise businesses in your community.

  A. _____
  B. _____
  C. _____

7. If you were starting a business, would you rather start a one-of-a-kind business or a franchise business? Explain. _____

8. What kinds of service businesses do you patronize?_____

9. List five service businesses in your community and identify the type of service provided by each.

Business	Service
A. _____	_____
B. _____	_____
C. _____	_____
D. _____	_____
E. _____	_____

10. If you started a service business, what type of service would you like to provide? _____
_____

11. Why would you want to provide this type of service? _____
_____

12. Why do you think people would be willing to pay for your service? _____

Is Entrepreneurship for You?

Activity C   **Name** _____

Chapter 6   **Date** _____ **Period** _____

Answer the following questions to help determine if becoming an entrepreneur is a profession that appeals to you. (Student response.)

1. Which of the following goals do you have for your career? (Check all that apply.)

    _____ To make a lot of money.
    _____ To do your job better than another company or person.
    _____ To develop a new idea.
    _____ To be your own boss.
    _____ To set your own working hours.
    _____ To make your own decisions.
    _____ To gain recognition in the community.

2. Answer the following questions by checking either the Yes or No column.

	Yes	No
A. Do you have a good imagination?	_____	_____
B. Do you think you could manage a business successfully?	_____	_____
C. Do you often think of creative ways to solve problems?	_____	_____
D. Do you have a lot of ambition and drive?	_____	_____
E. Do you have a good knowledge of a product you would like to sell or a service you would like to provide?	_____	_____
F. Can you make decisions?	_____	_____
G. Can you supervise people well?	_____	_____
H. Can you motivate people to do their work well?	_____	_____
I. Are you comfortable around people you don't know?	_____	_____

3. Which of the following aspects of entrepreneurship would discourage you from starting your own business? (Check all that apply.)

    _____ long working hours
    _____ high level of stress
    _____ financial risk

4. What would you consider to be the biggest advantage of owning your own business? Explain.

    _____

    _____

5. What would you consider to be the biggest disadvantage of owning your own business? Explain.

    _____

    _____

6. Do you think you would like to be an entrepreneur? Explain._____

    _____

    _____

Business Advice

Activity D   **Name** _____

Chapter 6   **Date** _____ **Period** _____

Find out the answers to the questions below by inviting an entrepreneur to class or interviewing a friend or relative who is an independent businessperson.   (Student response.)

Entrepreneur's name: _____

Type of business: _____

1. What kinds of products or services do you offer? _____

2. How long have you been in business? _____
   _____

3. What type of business organization do you have (sole proprietorship, partnership, or corporation)? Why did you choose that type of organization? _____

4. When did you first consider becoming an entrepreneur? _____

5. What was your main reason for wanting to start your own business? _____
   _____

6. Give a brief history of your business. _____
   _____
   _____
   _____
   _____

7. If you were starting over today, what would you do differently? _____
   _____

8. If you were starting over today, what would you do the same? _____
   _____

9. What is the biggest challenge of owning your own business? _____
   _____
   _____

10. What do you feel are the most important characteristics for an entrepreneur to have? _____ ___
    _____

11. What advice would you offer to someone who is considering becoming an entrepreneur? _____
    _____
    _____
    _____
    _____
    _____

Planning a Business

Activity E   Name _____

Chapter 6   Date _____ Period _____

You don't have to be an adult to be an entrepreneur! Complete this activity to plan a business you could start right now while in school. (Student response.)

1. What type of business do you want? _____

2. List any hobbies, classes, part-time jobs, or other accomplishments that provided you with some experience in this type of business. _____

   _____

3. What will you call your business? _____

4. Who will your customers be? (Consider age, sex, lifestyle, and any other characteristics that might encourage interest in your products or services.) _____

   _____

5. In the chart below, list all the equipment and supplies needed to start your business. Specify how many of each item you would need. For each item listed, check the appropriate column to indicate whether you would borrow it, buy it used, or buy it new. Estimate a cost for each item you would need to buy.

Item	Borrow	Buy Used	Buy New	Estimated Cost
			Total	

6. Can you run this business from your home? If not, where would you locate your business? _____

   _____

   How much will it cost? _____

7. How will you advertise your business? _____

   How much will it cost? _____

8. Can you run this business by yourself? _____

   If not, who will help you? _____

   _____

   How much will this cost? _____

(Continued)

Name _____

9. Use the cost information from items 5 through 8 to estimate your total expenses for one week.

_____

10. In the first column of the chart below, list the products or services that you believe will be your biggest moneymakers. In the second column, estimate how many of each product you will sell or how many times you will provide each service per week. In the third column, indicate how much you plan to charge for each product or service. Enter your total estimated income from each item in the last column. (Find this by multiplying the second and third columns for each item.)

Product or Service	Number per Week	Cost per Item	Income per Item
		Total Income per Week	

11. Subtract your estimate of total expenses per week (#9) from your estimate of total income per week (#10).

_____ − _____ = _____

Will you make a profit or suffer a loss?_____

12. Would you like to put this plan into action? Explain._____

_____

_____

_____

_____

_____

_____

_____

_____

_____

_____

_____

_____

_____

_____

_____

_____

_____

Business Organizations

Activity F

Chapter 6

Name _____

Date _____   Period _____

Use information from the chapter and library resources to investigate the different types of business organizations. Complete the chart below, listing the advantages and disadvantages of each type of organization. Then answer the questions that follow.

Type of Organization	Advantages	Disadvantages
Sole Proprietorship	It is the easiest type of business to start and dissolve because no other owners are involved. The owner makes all business decisions, does most of the work, and earns all the profits.	Being the owner means you are responsible for all bills and expenses. If the business fails, the owner's personal property may be taken to cover any outstanding debts.
Partnership	Partners combine their money and energy. They often share the work, responsibilities, debts, and profits. Ideas can be shared and problems can be discussed before making decisions. If the business fails, the losses are shared with the partners.	One of the partners may feel that he or she is being treated unfairly. Partners may disagree on how to run the business. Such feelings can cause partnerships to fail.
Corporation	Selling stock in a company provides a greater amount of money to the business. This type of organization offers some different legal and tax advantages than a partnership or sole proprietorship.	Stockholders risk the amount of their original stock investment if the business fails.

If you were starting a business, which type of business organization would you use? Explain.

(Student response.) _____

_____

_____

_____

_____

(Continued)

Name _____

Would you ever consider changing your business to another type of organization once it became successful? Explain.

____(Student response.)_____

_____

_____

_____

_____

_____

_____

_____

Is there a type of business organization you definitely would not use? Explain.

____(Student response.)_____

_____

_____

_____

_____

_____

_____

_____

_____

Learning About Yourself

Reinforcing Vocabulary

Activity A

Chapter 7

Name _____

Date _____ Period _____

Match the following terms with the correct definitions. Also give examples where requested.

___F___ 1. All the items or qualities you have or can use to help you get what you want.
Give two examples:

_____

_____

___E___ 2. The group of traits that makes each person unique.
Name two common traits:

_____

_____

___G___ 3. What you know and feel about yourself.

___C___ 4. How you react to a situation.

___B___ 5. Natural talents and the potential to learn easily and quickly.
Give two examples:

_____

_____

___A___ 6. Skills you can develop and improve.
Give two examples:

_____

_____

___H___ 7. Beliefs, ideas, or objects that are important to you.
Give two examples:

_____

_____

___D___ 8. The ideas, subjects, or activities you enjoy.

(Examples are student response.)

A. abilities
B. aptitudes
C. attitude
D. interests
E. personality
F. resources
G. self-concept
H. values

Your Personality Traits and Self-Concept

Activity B

Chapter 7

Name _____

Date _____ Period _____

Personality traits are among the resources that can help you choose a career you will like. Evaluate your personality traits by placing a check in the blanks near the statements that describe you. (Student response.)

_____ 1. I like to work.
_____ 2. I am trustworthy.
_____ 3. I am often late to school.
_____ 4. I accept criticism and try to make improvements.
_____ 5. I am sure of myself.
_____ 6. I brag a lot.
_____ 7. I usually arrive at school early.
_____ 8. I am always willing to help others.
_____ 9. I only do things I like.
_____ 10. I am polite.
_____ 11. Before offering to help, I usually ask myself, "What's in it for me?"
_____ 12. I don't like being told what to do.
_____ 13. I am sometimes impolite.
_____ 14. I do only what I have to do to get along.
_____ 15. I like to work ahead.
_____ 16. I am almost always careful to do things right.
_____ 17. I am willing to work hard for what I want.
_____ 18. I need little direction to get jobs done.
_____ 19. I'd rather watch TV than go to school or work.
_____ 20. I believe telling a lie is sometimes better than telling the truth.
_____ 21. I don't believe I should have to work hard.
_____ 22. I'm often unsure of myself and my decisions.
_____ 23. I'm ambitious.
_____ 24. I'm often sloppy about my appearance.
_____ 25. I ignore things I don't like.
_____ 26. I like responsibility.
_____ 27. I like to please people.
_____ 28. I am almost always neat about my appearance.
_____ 29. I am often impatient with others.
_____ 30. I have trouble following directions.

From the list of traits you checked, identify the five that you believe are your best resources. Explain how each of these traits would be helpful in a career.

1. _____
2. _____
3. _____
4. _____
5. _____

(Continued)

Name _____

Identify three traits you need to change—either positive traits you need to develop or negative traits you need to adjust. Explain why changing each of these traits would be helpful in a career.

1. _____

2. _____

3. _____

Describe your self-concept.

_____

_____

_____

_____

_____

_____

_____

_____

Explain how your self-concept can affect your chances of getting and keeping a job.

_____

_____

_____

_____

_____

_____

_____

_____

Identifying My Interests—People, Data, Objects

Activity C

Chapter 7

Name _____

Date _____ Period _____

To choose a career that you will enjoy, you must first know your interests. What do you like to do? Identify five activities you enjoy that focus on each of the following: people, data, and objects. Then answer the questions that follow. (Sample responses.)

People

Are you a "people" person? Do you like to join clubs, help others, give instructions, influence decisions, or plan social events? List five activities you enjoy that focus on people.

1. coaching younger children
2. visiting people at a retirement home
3. working as an usher at a theatre
4. giving parties for my friends
5. attending student council meetings

Data (Ideas)

Are you a "data" person? Do you enjoy gathering information, working with numbers, maintaining records, and keeping track of details? List five activities you enjoy that focus on data.

1. balancing my checkbook
2. doing inventory at work
3. working number puzzles
4. keeping score at a game
5. doing research for a project

Objects (Things)

Are you a "things" person? Do you enjoy repairing items, operating machines, using tools, working on crafts, or gardening? List five activities you enjoy that focus on tools, machines, or other objects.

1. growing vegetables
2. fixing my bike
3. woodworking
4. cooking
5. playing guitar

(Continued)

Name _____

Do your favorite interests focus on people, data, or objects? (If your favorite interests fall into two categories, name both.) _People, Objects_____

_____

Of the 15 interests you listed on these two pages, which three do you enjoy most? List your favorite one first.

Interest #1:_giving parties for my friends_____

Interest #2:_cooking_____

Interest #3:_playing guitar_____

What career possibilities relate to your three top interests?

Career(s) related to Interest #1:_Event planner, Convention manager_____

_____

Career(s) related to Interest #2:_Caterer, Chef_____

_____

Career(s) related to Interest #3:_Entertainer, Musician_____

_____

Aptitudes, Abilities, and Values

Activity D   Name _____

Chapter 7   Date _____ Period _____

Define *aptitude*, *ability*, and *values* in the spaces provided. Then provide an example of one of the three qualities for each category listed below. Identify whether each example is an aptitude, ability, or value. The first example is provided for you.

Definitions

Aptitude: _A natural talent a person has or the potential to learn certain skills easily and quickly._

_____

Ability: _A skill a person has developed._

_____

Value: _A belief, idea, or object that is important to an individual._

_____

(Sample responses.)

1. An example of a(n) <u>value</u> involving **family** is: eating dinners together every night to promote family unity and communication.

2. An example of a(n) _____ability_____ involving **public speaking** is:_____
   after much research, earning a good score at a regional debate meet.

3. An example of a(n) _____value_____ involving **education** is:_____
   saving money to finance further education.

4. An example of a(n) _____aptitude_____ involving **sports** is:_____
   winning tennis matches with little effort.

5. An example of a(n) _____ability_____ involving a **musical instrument** is: _____
   playing a difficult piece on the piano after lots of practice.

6. An example of a(n) _____aptitude_____ involving **painting or some other fine art** is: _____
   being able to paint a portrait easily.

7. An example of a(n) _____ability_____ involving a **computer** is: _____
   knowing and using many programs efficiently.

8. An example of a(n) _____ability_____ involving **science** is:_____
   being able to conduct experiments accurately.

9. An example of a(n) _____value_____ involving **friends** is: _____
   making time to be with them and making them feel special.

10. An example of a(n) _____value_____ involving **time** is: _____
    preparing a schedule to make the best use of it.

Making Decisions

Reinforcing Vocabulary

Activity A

Chapter 8

Name _____

Date _____ Period _____

Read each of the definitions below and decide which chapter term is being defined. Write the correct term in the crossword puzzle.

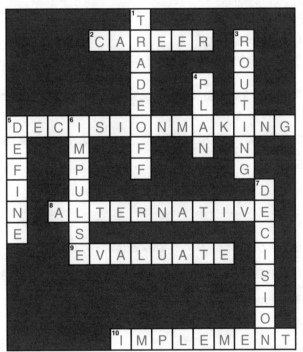

Across

2. Personal decisions may also affect _____ decisions.
5. The _____-_____ process is the seven-step guide for making choices based on careful thinking and planning.
8. A(n) _____ is a choice or option when making a decision.
9. After making a decision, it is important to _____ the results.
10. To _____ is to put a plan into action.

Down

1. A(n) _____ occurs when one thing is given up in return for another.
3. Decisions that are made often and automatically are _____ decisions.
4. The sixth step of the decision-making process is to develop a _____ of action.
5. The first step in making a decision is to _____ the decision to be made.
6. A decision that is made based on feelings or reactions to a situation is a(n) _____ decision.
7. Making a(n) _____ means making a choice or a judgment.

The Decision-Making Process

Activity B

Chapter 8

Name _____

Date _____ Period _____

Match the following thoughts about deciding what to wear with the correct steps of the decision-making process. Then answer the questions that follow.

_____D_____ 1. The sweater looks great on me, but I sometimes get too warm when I wear it. The flannel shirt looks old and faded. It also fits rather snugly. The sweatshirt looks casual, but neat. It is very comfortable.

_____B_____ 2. I usually make good choices. I can listen to the weather forecast.

_____G_____ 3. It turned out to be warmer today than I expected. I would have been warm in the sweater and uncomfortable in the tight flannel shirt. Wearing the sweatshirt was a good decision.

_____F_____ 4. I will wear the sweatshirt.

_____C_____ 5. A sweater, a flannel shirt, a sweatshirt.

_____A_____ 6. What should I wear to school?

_____E_____ 7. The sweatshirt would be the best choice.

(Sample responses.)

A. Define the issue.

B. Make a self-inventory.

C. List all possible alternatives.

D. Forecast the outcome of each alternative.

E. Choose the best alternative.

F. Develop a plan of action.

G. Evaluate the results.

Choose one of the steps of the decision-making process. Explain what might happen if you fail to take that step when making an important decision.

List all possible alternatives. You won't be able to weigh all of your options.

_____

_____

_____

When is it most helpful to use the decision-making process? Explain.

It is most helpful to use the decision-making process when making difficult or important decisions

because it helps you to sort through your thoughts.

_____

_____

Describe situations when it would not be worthwhile to use the decision-making process.

It would not be worthwhile to use the decision-making process when making routine or impulse

decisions such as what to wear or what movie to see.

_____

_____

Give an example of how the decision-making process could be used at work.

The decision-making process could be used at work in deciding to work overtime if given that option.

_____

_____

Trade-Offs

Activity C

Chapter 8

Name _____

Date _____ **Period** _____

For every decision you make, there are trade-offs. Read the decisions listed below and describe one trade-off for each decision. (Sample responses.)

1. To lose 10 pounds in a month

   I would have to give up pizza and sweets. _____

   _____

2. To get a driver's license within two weeks

   I would have to spend time studying for the test rather than going to the mall. _____

   _____

3. To go to Europe on spring break

   I would miss my brother's birthday party. _____

   _____

4. To get a job immediately after graduating from high school

   I would give up the opportunity to go to college. _____

   _____

5. To make the honor roll next grading period

   I would have to spend many extra hours studying. _____

   _____

6. To play a video game after school

   I would give up spending time playing with my dog. _____

   _____

7. To save $4,000 in one year for a car

   I would have to give up a spring break trip to Europe. _____

   _____

8. To learn to dance in four weeks

   I would need to spend most of my free time practicing. _____

   _____

9. To buy a new outfit this month

   I would have to skip a trip to the amusement park. _____

   _____

10. To complete all homework during study periods at school

    I would have to do less socializing with friends. _____

    _____

Preparing for Career Decisions

Activity D   Name _____

Chapter 8   Date _____ Period _____

Planning ahead is the key to making a satisfying career decision. By starting to think about a career now, you will be better prepared to make decisions in the future. Start planning for your career by answering the following questions. (Student response.)

1. What courses and programs will you take in high school? _____

   _____

   _____

   _____

   _____

   _____

   _____

2. How much effort will you put into your studies? _____

   _____

   _____

   _____

   _____

   _____

3. What skills will you develop? _____

   _____

   _____

   _____

   _____

   _____

4. What education and training beyond high school do you want to pursue? _____

   _____

   _____

   _____

5. What careers will you explore? _____

   _____

   _____

   _____

Making Decisions at Work

Activity E　　　　　　　　　　　**Name** _____

Chapter 8　　　　　　　　　　　**Date** _____ **Period** _____

Some decisions at work are easy to make, but other decisions require more careful thought. The more you practice making those difficult decisions, the easier they will become. Read the case studies that follow and answer the questions to complete the decision-making process. (Sample responses.)

Case Study I

Jeannie has just begun a new job as an air conditioning and heating technician's assistant. Jeannie's job is to get the tools ready for her boss. She is also expected to clean up the work area at the end of the day. During the day, other workers ask Jeannie to get materials for them. She helps stock supplies at the job site. Sometimes Jeannie does errands for the senior technicians on the job.

Jeannie's work area is often left dirty at the end of the day. Sometimes she keeps her boss from leaving work on time. She is often late in putting away the equipment. Lately, her supervisor has been reprimanding her quite often. Jeannie may not get a raise at the next salary review if her work has not improved.

1. What decision does Jeannie have to make? Jeannie has to decide how to become better organized and make better use of her time.

2. What are her alternatives? She can work with her supervisor to find out how to work more efficiently. She can ask for an assistant. She can do nothing to improve.

3. What are the trade-offs for each alternative? If she chooses the first alternative, she will have to work harder. If she chooses the second alternative she could get her portion of the job done. If she chooses the third alternative, she won't have to work as hard.

4. What is the probable outcome of each alternative? The probable outcome of the first alternative would be that she would become more organized and that she might get a raise. The probable outcome of the second alternative is that she may be seen as not capable of handling the job. The probable outcome of the third alternative might be that she would not get a raise and/or be fired.

5. What decision would you make if you were in Jeannie's place? (Student response.)

6. Why would you make this decision? (Student response.)

(Continued)

Name _____

Case Study II

Henry is a senior in a cooperative education program. He has been working for four weeks as a word processor in an office. Henry is one of six cooperative education students employed by the firm. Henry has much better office skills than the other students.

It is time for Ms. Jacobs, Henry's boss, to evaluate him and determine his continued employment. She has reviewed his file and has found that Henry does far more work than any of the other students. However, she has also noted that Henry is nearly 15 minutes late every day.

When talking to Henry, Ms. Jacobs once asked Henry why he was late every day. Henry replied, "I do more work than any other part-time worker here. I don't think it should matter if I come in late. I get the same pay and do more work. It's not fair that I work as long as the others."

Ms. Jacobs sees Henry's lateness as a serious problem. She is afraid the other students will begin to come in late if Henry continues to do so. On the other hand, she sees Henry's skills as an asset to the company.

1. What decision does Henry's boss have to make? _She has to decide whether to hire Henry._

   _____

   _____

2. What are her alternatives? _She can hire him. She can work with him to solve his problem and_
   attitude about being late, and then hire him. She can refuse to hire him.

   _____

   _____

3. What are the trade-offs for each alternative? _She can hire him, but she'd have to deal with his_
   attitude and those other employees might adopt. She could spend the time and effort to solve the
   problem. If she didn't hire him she wouldn't have to deal with his attitude, but lose his skills.

   _____

   _____

4. What is the probable outcome of each alternative? _If she hires him, his skills would be an asset,_
   however, his poor attitude would continue and other students may come in late. If she works with
   him to solve his problem and attitude about being late, it may take time, but she would have a
   valuable employee. If she refuses to hire him, she will lose his skills.

   _____

   _____

5. What decision would you make if you were Henry's boss? _(Student response.)_

   _____

   _____

   _____

6. Why would you make this decision? _(Student response.)_

   _____

   _____

   _____

Options for Education and Training

Reinforcing Vocabulary

Activity A	**Name** _____
Chapter 9	**Date** _____ **Period** _____

Match the following terms with their correct definitions.

___K___   1. Training offered by the U.S. Government for members of the Navy, Army, Air Force, Marines, or Coast Guard.

___H___   2. Training program that prepares employees to do a specialized job within their company.

___D___   3. Skills, such as reading, writing, and math, which are required for any career.

___A___   4. Training that involves learning a trade by working under the direction and guidance of a skilled worker.

___B___   5. Degree usually received after completing two years of education beyond high school.

___E___   6. Programs in the areas of health, business, agriculture, skilled trades, and marketing that may be offered to students who are still in high school.

___C___   7. Degree usually received after completing a four-year program beyond high school.

___I___   8. An arrangement between schools and places of employment that allows students to receive on-the-job training.

___G___   9. Institutions of higher learning that offer an associate degree.

___F___   10. Institutions of higher learning that offer bachelor's, master's, and doctorate degrees.

___J___   11. A student seeking skills for a career, who works in a temporary position with an emphasis on on-the-job training rather than employment.

A. apprenticeship
B. associate degree
C. bachelor's degree
D. basic skills
E. career/technical training
F. colleges and universities
G. community and junior college
H. company training program
I. cooperative education
J. intern
K. military training

Basic Skills for the Workplace

Activity B   Name _____

Chapter 9   Date _____ Period _____

Basic reading, writing, and math skills are necessary in all jobs. To be a successful worker, you will need these skills as well as occupational skills. Complete the charts below by identifying two occupations that interest you. List the tasks that you think people do in those occupations and the basic skills needed for those tasks. Then decide whether you have the skills needed to perform those tasks. (Sample responses.)

Occupation 1: _Financial Analyst_____

Tasks	**Basic Skills Needed**
1. analyze data	reading, math
2. prepare budgets	math
3. develop financial forecasts	reading, writing, math

Do you have the skills needed to perform the tasks listed above? If not, what can you do now to develop the skills? (Student response.) _____

_____

_____

_____

Occupation 2: _Physical Therapist_____

Tasks	**Basic Skills Needed**
1. examine patients' medical histories	reading
2. measure patients' strength and range of motion	math
3. develop plans describing treatment strategies	writing

Do you have the skills needed to perform the tasks listed above? If not, what can you do now to develop the skills? (Student response.) _____

_____

_____

_____

Plans for Career Training

Activity C

Chapter 9

Name _____

Date _____   Period _____

Many different forms of career training are available, but the best training for you depends on your personal career goals. Name a career area that interests you. Then, for each type of training program listed below, identify the different employment opportunities within your career area that you would be qualified to pursue. (Sample responses.)

Student's career interest: Construction _____

Apprenticeships:

Carpenter, Plumber _____

_____

_____

Four-year colleges and universities:

Architect, Regional and Urban Planner _____

_____

_____

Two-year community and junior colleges:

Drafter, Air Conditioning and Refrigeration Technician _____

_____

_____

Cooperative education:

Carpet Installer, Security and Fire Alarm Systems Installer _____

_____

_____

Internships:

Education and Training, Estimator _____

_____

_____

Military training:

Facilities Engineer, Project Inspector _____

_____

_____

Career/technical programs:

Landscaper, Mason _____

_____

_____

Figuring Education and Training Costs

Activity D   **Name** _____
Chapter 9   **Date** _____ **Period** _____

Use this form to estimate the cost of higher education. Choose a program of study that interests you and is offered at a nearby school. Contact the school to learn about the program and related school costs. Then answer the following questions. (Answers are student response.)

1. What program interests you? _____

_____

2. At which nearby school would you take this program? _____

_____

3. What is the address of the school? _____

_____

4. Would you live at home, on school property, or some other location? _____

_____

5. What would room and board cost for the first year? _____

_____

6. Would you travel to school via public transportation? (If no, how would you get to school?) _____

_____

7. What travel costs do you estimate for the first year? (If travel involves the purchase or lease of an automobile, include purchase/lease costs, insurance, taxes, parking fees, and all other associated costs.)

_____

_____

8. How much would you budget for clothing for one year? _____

9. How much would you budget for health care for one year? _____

10. How much would you budget for recreational activities for one year? _____

11. What are the **estimated related costs** (total of Questions 5–10)? _____

12. What is the cost of one-year's tuition? _____

13. Are there any special program fees? _____

14. Are there any required student fees? _____

15. What will schoolbooks and school supplies cost for the first year? _____

_____

16. What is the **estimated school cost** (total of Questions 12–15)? _____

17. What is the **estimated first-year cost** for advanced education (total of Questions 11 and 16)? _____

_____

18. Of the many options open to you, how would you pay for the first year of advanced education? _____

_____

_____

Chapter 10
Making a Career Plan

Reinforcing Vocabulary

Activity A

Chapter 10

Name _____

Date _____ Period _____

Fill in the blanks with the correct chapter terms. Then give examples where requested.

1. _____Human_____ resources are qualities or abilities that people have within themselves that can help them achieve goals. Two examples are the following: _____

   (Sample response.) determination, ambition _____

   _____

2. _____Nonhuman_____ resources are material resources that can help people achieve goals. Two examples are the following: _(Sample response.) money, time_ _____

   _____

3. _____Goals_____ are aims or targets a person tries to reach or achieve.
   A _____long-term_____ _____goal_____ is an aim or target that will take more than six months to accomplish. Two examples are the following: _____

   (Sample response.) going to college, planning a trip around the world _____

   _____

4. A _____short-term_____ _____goal_____ is a target that can be accomplished within a few days, weeks, or months. Two examples are the following: _____

   (Sample response.) saving enough money to buy a computer _____

   _____

5. A _____personal_____ _____goal_____ is something you want to achieve for yourself.
   Two examples are the following: _(Sample response.) to get good grades, to graduate_ _____

   _____

6. A _____professional_____ _____goal_____ is a target you want to reach in your career. Two examples might be the following: _____

   (Sample response.) to get an entry-level job in banking, to become a manager within five years

7. A _____career_____ _____plan_____ is a list of steps you need to take to reach your career goal. It should include the following three items: _____

   A. _extracurricular and volunteer activities_ _____

   B. _entry-level jobs_ _____

   C. _education and training requirements_ _____

Job Likes and Dislikes

Activity B

Chapter 10

Name _____

Date _____ Period _____

Knowing your strong likes and dislikes will help you make a good career choice. Use the following checklist to see what kinds of jobs you would like most. If you would like the work situation described, place a check in the *likes* column. If you would not like the work described, place a check in the *dislikes* column.

(Checklist is student response.)

Likes	Dislikes	
_____	_____	1. Work with many people
_____	_____	2. Talk to people at work
_____	_____	3. Work alone
_____	_____	4. Work inside
_____	_____	5. Work outside
_____	_____	6. Repair or make things
_____	_____	7. Work at one place
_____	_____	8. Travel to many worksites
_____	_____	9. Work regular hours
_____	_____	10. Work varied hours
_____	_____	11. Work days
_____	_____	12. Work nights
_____	_____	13. Work while standing or walking
_____	_____	14. Work while sitting
_____	_____	15. Work in a quiet place
_____	_____	16. Handle physical work
_____	_____	17. Handle mental work
_____	_____	18. Work with heavy machinery
_____	_____	19. Work with office equipment
_____	_____	20. Work in areas that may be dirty
_____	_____	21. Work in areas that are always clean
_____	_____	22. Work close to home
_____	_____	23. Work in a secure job
_____	_____	24. Work in a job that requires personal risks or challenges
_____	_____	25. Work in a job that will provide recognition by many people
_____	_____	26. Work for a large company
_____	_____	27. Work for a small company
_____	_____	28. Work in a job that requires special training
_____	_____	29. Work in a job that requires no special training
_____	_____	30. Work in a job free of hazards
_____	_____	31. Work in a job that may sometimes be dangerous
_____	_____	32. Work in a job that involves children
_____	_____	33. Work in a job that helps people
_____	_____	34. Work in a job that teaches/instructs people
_____	_____	35. Work in a job that informs people
_____	_____	36. Work in a job that sells goods
_____	_____	37. Work in a large city
_____	_____	38. Work in a small city or town
_____	_____	39. Work in a rural setting

(Continued)

Name _____

Based on the checklist on the previous page, describe the type of job you want._____

___(Description is student response.)_____

_____

_____

_____

_____

_____

_____

_____

_____

_____

_____

_____

_____

_____

_____

_____

_____

_____

_____

_____

_____

_____

_____

_____

_____

_____

_____

_____

Career Interests and Abilities Inventory

Activity C
Chapter 10

Name _____

Date _____ Period _____

Your interests and abilities can lead you to a career that will be fun and exciting for you. List three of your interests or abilities that relate to each area below. Then list one job you might like based on each interest or ability. (Inventory is student response.)

My Interests and Abilities	Related Jobs I Might Like
Hobbies	
1. _____	1. _____
2. _____	2. _____
3. _____	3. _____
Leisure activities	
1. _____	1. _____
2. _____	2. _____
3. _____	3. _____
Favorite school subjects	
1. _____	1. _____
2. _____	2. _____
3. _____	3. _____
Part-time or volunteer work	
1. _____	1. _____
2. _____	2. _____
3. _____	3. _____
Special abilities	
1. _____	1. _____
2. _____	2. _____
3. _____	3. _____

Setting and Reaching Goals

Activity D   **Name** _____

Chapter 10   **Date** _____ **Period** _____

You make things happen by setting goals and making plans for reaching them. Think about your goals by completing this activity. Your responses will not be graded. (Answers are student response.)

1. List five goals you would like to accomplish within the next few months.

    A. _____

    _____

    B. _____

    _____

    C. _____

    _____

    D. _____

    _____

    E. _____

    _____

2. List five goals you would like to accomplish within the next five to ten years.

    A. _____

    _____

    B. _____

    _____

    C. _____

    _____

    D. _____

    _____

    E. _____

    _____

(Continued)

Name _____

3. Select the one goal from each list that is most important to you. Write these two goals in the space provided. Use checks to show whether each goal is personal or professional and short-term or long-term.

Most Important Goals	Professional Goal	Short-Term Goal	Long-Term Goal	Personal Goal
A.				
B.				

4. Select the one goal that is most important to you and write it as a statement. Indicate the date you want to reach this goal.

_____

_____

_____

_____

5. Decide how you will reach your goal and write a detailed plan.

_____

_____

_____

_____

_____

_____

_____

_____

_____

_____

_____

_____

_____

_____

_____

_____

_____

_____

Chapter 11
Job Search Skills

Reinforcing Vocabulary

Activity A

Chapter 11

Name _____

Date _____ **Period** _____

Write each of the following terms from the chapter in the blank in front of its definition.

closed ad
electronic bulletin boards
job application form
networking
open ad
portfolio

private employment agency
public employment service
references
résumé
want ads

private employment agency	1. A business that helps people find jobs for a fee.
public employment service	2. A government-supported group that helps people find jobs for free.
electronic bulletin board	3. These allow you to post and read messages on the computer, acting as a media for the exchange of information among large groups of people, combining the features of electronic mail with private computer conferencing.
résumé	4. A formal written summary of a person's education, work experience, and other qualifications for a job.
references	5. People who can speak about a person's character and skills.
portfolio	6. A selection of materials that you can use to document your accomplishments over a period of time.
job application	7. A form completed by a job applicant to provide an employer with information about the applicant's background.
want ad	8. A source of information about available jobs, found in the classified section of the newspaper.
open ad	9. A classified ad providing specific information about a job.
closed ad	10. A classified ad giving general information about a job.
networking	11. Checking with family, friends, and other people you know to find out about job openings.

Want Ad Abbreviations

Activity B

Chapter 11

Name _____

Date _____ Period _____

Many want ads use abbreviations to save space. Study the abbreviations listed in Figure 11-2 of the text. Then read each ad below and write out the entire ad without using abbreviations. Use a dictionary to look up any unfamiliar abbreviations.

1.
> Temp., p/t help wanted. No exp. nec., co. will train. Some eve. hrs., good sal., light wk. Call 555-1212.

Temporary, part-time help wanted. No experience necessary, company will train. Some evening

hours, good salary, light work. Call 555-1212.

_____

_____

_____

2.
> F/T ofc. wk., oppty. to grow into mgr. position. Some bkkg. exp. nec., keyboard 50 wpm. Call Ms. Jones between 9 a.m. and 3 p.m. at 555-6677.

Full-time office work, opportunity to grow into manager position. Some bookkeeping experience

necessary, keyboard 50 words per minute. Call Ms. Jones between 9:00 a.m. and 3:00 p.m.

at 555-6677.

_____

_____

3.
> Immed. opening for asst. mgr. Ex. benefits, sal. neg. Refs. & 5 yrs. exp. req. (EOE) Joe's Fast Foods, call Mr. Banks 555-6273.

Immediate opening for assistant manager. Excellent benefits, salary negotiable. References and

five years experience required. Equal opportunity employer. Joe's Fast Foods, call Mr. Banks

at 555-6273.

_____

_____

Using Want Ads

Activity C

Chapter 11

Name _____

Date _____ Period _____

Find the classified section in your local newspaper and locate the want ads. Find an ad that matches your interests and level of education and mount it in the space below. Use the ad to answer the questions that follow.

(Student response based on ad supplied by student.)

1. What is the title of the advertised job? _____

2. What salary is listed or expected for this job? _____

3. What education is required for this job? _____

_____

4. What job requirements are listed? _____

_____

_____

5. What strengths do you possess for this job? _____

_____

6. Whom should you contact for further information concerning this job? _____

_____

7. What further training might you need for this job? _____

_____

_____

8. How can you get more information about the company before you make contact with them?_____

_____

_____

9. What questions should you be prepared to answer when you make contact with the company? _____

_____

_____

_____

10. What additional information about this job would you request? _____

_____

_____

Résumé Worksheet

Activity D
Chapter 11

Name _____

Date _____ Period _____

Develop your own résumé by filling in the information requested. Follow the guidelines given in the text. You may include optional information if you wish. Ask a friend or relative to read over your résumé and give you suggestions. Then type or neatly print your final résumé on your own paper.   (Student response.)

Name: _____

Address: _____

Telephone number: _____

Employment:

_____
_____
_____
_____
_____
_____

Education:

_____
_____
_____
_____
_____
_____

Activities and Honors:

_____
_____
_____

Hobbies:

_____
_____

References:

_____
_____
_____
_____
_____

Applying for Employment

Activity E   Name _____

Chapter 11   Date _____ Period _____

Complete this application for employment. Print clearly and fill in all the requested information. Apply for an employment opportunity in your interest area. (Student response based on information provided on pages 210-211 of the text.)

APPLICATION FOR EMPLOYMENT

PERSONAL INFORMATION

Name_____

      Last   First   Middle

Present Address _____

               Street   City   State   Zip

Telephone _____

       Area

JOB INTEREST

Position for which you are applying: _____

Salary desired: _____ Date you can start: _____

Have you ever been employed by this company before? _____

If yes, where? _____ When? _____

EDUCATION AND TRAINING

Name and Address of School	Number of Years Completed	Major Studies
Grade School		
High School		
Trade or Business School		
College		

EMPLOYMENT RECORD

Name and Address of Employers Beginning with Your Most Recent Employer	Type of Work	Dates Employed	Reason for Leaving

(Continued)

Name _____

If you have served in the U.S. Armed Forces, indicate:

Branch _____   Special Training _____

Rank Attained _____   Years in Service _____

Honors or Awards _____   Date of Separation _____

REFERENCES (List the names of three people not related to you whom you have known at least one year.)

Name	Address	Phone Number	Occupation	Years Known

ADDITIONAL DATA

Have you ever been convicted of a crime (other than traffic, game law, or other minor violations)? _____

If yes, explain the offense and circumstances regarding the conviction: _____

Is your age under 18? _____

Are you a U.S. Citizen? _____

If no, do you have an alien registration card or valid U.S. work permit? _____

Non-English languages you read _____ speak _____ write _____

Special skills, knowledge, and abilities that qualify you for the position you are seeking: _____

_____

_____

PHYSICAL STATUS

Are you presently or have you during the last six months been under a physician's care or in a hospital?

_____

Have you ever been compensated for, or do you currently have outstanding, a job-related claim? _____

If yes to any of the above, explain: _____

_____

Thank you for completing this application form and for your interest in employment with us. We would like to assure you that your opportunity for employment with this company will be based only on your merit without regard to your race, religion, sex, age, national origin, or disability.

PLEASE READ CAREFULLY
APPLICANT'S CERTIFICATION AND AGREEMENT

I certify that the facts contained in this application are true and complete to the best of my knowledge. I understand that, if employed, falsified statements on this application shall be grounds for dismissal.

I authorize investigation of all statements contained in this application. I authorize the references listed above to give you any and all information concerning my previous employment and any pertinent information they may have, personal or otherwise. I release all parties from all liability for any damage that may result from furnishing this information to you.

Date _____   Signature of applicant _____

Interviewing Skills

Reinforcing Vocabulary

Activity A

Chapter 12

Name _____

Date _____ Period _____

Match the following terms with their correct definitions.

C	1. A talk between an employer and a job applicant.	A. follow-up letter
E	2. The company representative who talks with job applicants.	B. job description
G	3. Telephone conversation between a company representative and a job applicant.	C. interview
F	4. Face-to-face meeting between an employer and a job applicant.	D. interviewee
B	5. An explanation of tasks to be performed by an employee in a specific position.	E. interviewer
A	6. A brief letter written in business form to thank the interviewer for the interview.	F. personal interview
D	7. A job applicant who receives an interview.	G. telephone interview

Write a one- or two-paragraph story about someone who is looking for a job. Correctly use all the above vocabulary terms in your story.

_____

_____

_____

_____

_____

_____

_____

_____

_____

_____

_____

_____

_____

_____

Company Research

Activity B

Chapter 12

Name _____

Date _____ Period _____

Select a company at which you would like to work and a job that you would like to have. Research the company and the job. Then provide the information requested below. (Student response.)

1. At what company would you like to work? _____

   _____

2. Why would you like to work there? _____

   _____

   _____

3. What job would you like to have? _____

4. Why do you think you would like this job? _____

   _____

   _____

5. What skills are needed for this job? _____

   _____

6. List any needed skills you are lacking and describe how you could acquire them. _____

   _____

   _____

7. What products does the company produce, or what services does it offer? _____

8. Have you ever used these products or services? If so, explain why you were or were not satisfied.___

   _____

9. How many people are employed by the company? _____

10. Does the company have plans for future growth or expansion?_____

11. What opportunities for advancement would be available to you?_____

    _____

12. List five questions you would ask if you were being interviewed for a job with this company. _____

    A. _____

       _____

    B. _____

       _____

    C. _____

       _____

    D. _____

       _____

    E. _____

       _____

Interview Questions

Activity C   **Name** _____
Chapter 12   **Date** _____ **Period** _____

Interviewers often ask job applicants the following questions. Answer each of the questions as though you were on a job interview. Discuss your answers in class.   (Student response.)

1. Why do you want to work here? _____
   _____
   _____

2. Tell me about yourself. _____
   _____
   _____
   _____
   _____

3. What are your favorite subjects in school? _____
   _____
   _____

4. What are your least favorite subjects in school? _____
   _____
   _____

5. What do you like to do in your free time? _____
   _____
   _____

6. Tell me about some of your other jobs. _____
   _____
   _____
   _____

7. Why did you leave your last job? _____
   _____
   _____

8. What are your major strengths? _____
   _____
   _____

9. What are your weaknesses? _____
   _____
   _____

10. What do you want to do five years from now? _____
    _____

Interview Practices

Activity D

Chapter 12

Name _____

Date _____ Period _____

Listed below are a variety of interview situations. Read each situation and decide whether the interview practice being described is a good practice or a poor one. In the blank space preceding each statement, either write *G* for good or *P* for poor. For those you mark *P*, use the space provided to explain what the interviewee should have done differently.

___P___ 1. As Glenn walked into the interviewer's office, he said, "I sure am tired. I gotta sit down and have a cigarette. Ya gotta light?"

Glenn should not have smoked during the interview. He should not have bothered the interviewer with how he felt. Glenn should not have sat down until asked. Glenn should have used standard English in speaking.

___G___ 2. William arrived for his interview 15 minutes early. After giving his name to the receptionist, he quietly waited until he was called for his interview.

___P___ 3. Because Jackie was babysitting her two-year-old brother, she brought him along to her interview.

Jackie should have come to the interview alone.

___P___ 4. After a fun day at the beach, Blake hurried to his interview at the drugstore wearing brightly colored shorts and no shirt.

Blake was not properly dressed for an interview at the drugstore. He should have allowed time to go home and change into casual pants and a shirt.

___P___ 5. When Joan interviewed at Hamburger Heaven, she said, "Ya know, I've eaten your hamburgers and they're really gross."

Joan should not have made a negative comment about the hamburgers. She also should have been careful not to use slang.

___G___ 6. When Katie interviewed for the receptionist's job, she said, "I don't have experience answering business phones, but I love talking with people and I'm willing to learn."

___P___ 7. Raymond was nervous at his first job interview. He looked at the wall instead of the interviewer and gave simple yes and no answers to the questions he was asked.

Raymond should have made eye contact with the interviewer even though he was nervous. He also should have given more than yes and no answers.

___G___ 8. Brian said to the interviewer, "I would do a good job as a groundskeeper for your company. For three years, I have had my own outdoor maintenance service, and all my customers have been satisfied."

(Continued)

Name _____

___P___ 9. The interviewer told Sally to make herself comfortable, so she sprawled out on the couch and began chewing bubble gum.
Sally should have sat up straight on the couch or a chair. She should not have chewed
bubble gum during the interview.

___G___ 10. Tom told the interviewer at A to Z Dry Cleaners that he and his family have always gotten excellent service there.
_____
_____

___G___ 11. Melanie said to the interviewer, "I want to be a candy striper because I like helping people and would like to become a nurse."
_____
_____

___G___ 12. Carla came to her interview for the typing position wearing a neatly pressed skirt and blouse.
_____
_____

___P___ 13. James told the interviewer, "I'm sorry I'm late, but I overslept."
James should have come to the interview on time. He should not have made excuses for
being late by saying he overslept.

___P___ 14. Marta said to the interviewer, "I'll take anything. I don't care what I do."
Marta should have told the interviewer the kind of work that interests her.
_____

___P___ 15. Amy said to the interviewer, "What hours would I work? I sleep until noon, so I can't get to work until 1 p.m."
Amy should not have told the interviewer she sleeps until noon. Unless she had a better
reason for not being able to work until 1 p.m., she should not have said anything.

Follow-Up in Writing

Activity E

Chapter 12

Name _____

Date _____ **Period** _____

Bob Johnson just completed an interview for a sales position with Joseph Sebastian, human resources manager for Watson's Department Store. Watson's is located at 735 S. River Road in Bently, Nebraska 00923. Bob lives nearby at 832 W. Roseville Drive in Bently.

Bob had heard he should send a follow-up letter after an interview, so he wrote the letter below. Bob had the right idea, but his letter needs a little work. Read his letter and answer the questions that follow.

Dear Joe,

Thanks for the interview. You seem like a nice guy, and the job sounded kinda fun. I wouldn't mind working for you. Let me know if I get the job.

Sincerely,

Bob Johnson

What suggestions would you give Bob for improving his letter?

Bob should have written the letter in business form, expressing his interest in the job. He should have

pointed out his qualifications for the job and politely requested to hear about the company's decision.

_____

Write a follow-up letter for Bob that might give Mr. Sebastian a better impression. (Use another sheet of paper if you need more space.)

(Follow-up letter is student response. Students should follow the format shown on page 226 in the text.)

_____

_____

_____

_____

_____

_____

_____

_____

_____

_____

_____

_____

_____

_____

Good Employee Skills

Reinforcing Vocabulary

Activity A

Chapter 13

Name _____

Date _____ Period _____

Read each of the definitions below and decide which chapter term is being defined. Write the correct terms in the crossword puzzle.

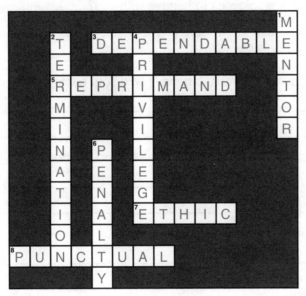

Across

3. Being reliable.
5. A _____ is a severe expression of disapproval.
7. A work _____ is a standard of conduct and values for job performance.
8. A person who is _____ comes to work on time.

Down

1. A more experienced person who provides his or her expertise in order to help less-experienced workers advance in their careers, enhance their education, and build networks.

2. The end of employment or the loss of a job is called _____.

4. A right that is given to an employee as a benefit or favor is a _____.

6. A _____ is a loss or hardship for breaking company rules and policies.

If You Were an Employer

Activity B

Chapter 13

Name _____

Date _____ Period _____

Imagine you are the owner of a small business. Answer the following questions about the expectations you would have for your employees. (Student response.)

1. What type of business would you own? _____

2. What traits would you want your employees to have? _____

_____

_____

3. How would you expect your employees to behave with one another? _____

_____

_____

4. How would you expect your employees to behave with you?_____

_____

_____

5. How would you expect your employees to behave with your customers and business contacts? _____

_____

_____

6. What kind of employees would you reward with raises and promotions? _____

_____

_____

7. What company rules and policies would you have for your employees? _____

_____

_____

_____

8. What kinds of penalties would you have for employees who broke your rules and policies?_____

_____

_____

9. Under what circumstances would you fire an employee? _____

_____

10. What time would you expect your employees to begin work each day?_____

11. What kinds of privileges would you extend to your employees? _____

12. Do you think your employees would enjoy working for you? Explain your answer. _____

_____

_____

Winners or Losers?

Activity C   Name _____

Chapter 13   Date _____ Period _____

Read the case studies below and answer the questions that follow.   (Student response. Suggested responses follow.)

Case I

Mary works as a data entry clerk for an insurance company. Mary has worked for the company for only a month. However, her boss is impressed with how quickly Mary has learned her job. She works hard and follows directions well.

Yesterday, while the receptionist was on her lunch break, Mary was helping out by answering the phone. She answered a call from a policyholder asking whether Mary's company planned to increase their rates this year. Trying to be helpful, Mary looked through the receptionist's desk. She found a file labeled, "New Rates—For Company Use ONLY." Mary opened the file and quoted the new rates to the caller.

1. What are Mary's winning work traits? Mary's winning work traits include learning quickly, working

    hard, following directions well, and being willing to help others.

    _____

    _____

2. What losing work traits does Mary need to improve? Mary needs to improve her apparent lack of

    respect for her coworkers, shown by looking through the receptionist's desk. She also needs to

    improve her judgment skills and loyalty to the company, shown by giving company information on

    prices to a policyholder.

Case II

Robert is a stock clerk at a local grocery store. Robert is proud of his job and of the store where he works. He never shops anywhere else, and he tells all his friends to shop there, too.

Robert does an excellent job of keeping the shelves of the store neat and clean and stocked with products. When Robert gets busy stocking, he doesn't like anything to interrupt him. In fact, the other day, the store manager heard Robert say to a customer, "Would you get out of my way, lady? Can't you see I'm trying to put these cans on the shelf?"

3. What are Robert's winning work traits? Robert's winning work traits include pride in his job, loyalty

    to the store, and excellence in his work.

    _____

    _____

4. What losing work traits does Robert need to improve? Robert needs to improve his attitude of

    service and his ability to get along with customers.

    _____

    _____

Winning Work Habits

Activity D   Name _____

Chapter 13   Date _____ Period _____

As you read each of the following statements about good work habits, decide whether your work habits are "on target" with the statement or "need improvement." Place a check in the column that best describes your work habits.   (Student response.)

On Target	Need Improvement	
_____	_____	1. I keep my work area neat and clean.
_____	_____	2. I respect materials, tools, and equipment.
_____	_____	3. I observe good health and safety practices.
_____	_____	4. I report to work on time.
_____	_____	5. I do not abuse work breaks.
_____	_____	6. I get along with my coworkers.
_____	_____	7. I carry out orders.
_____	_____	8. I take pride in my work and do it to the best of my ability.
_____	_____	9. I am eager to learn more about my job.
_____	_____	10. I have a good attendance record.
_____	_____	11. I don't waste time on the job.
_____	_____	12. I am eager to help others whenever I can.
_____	_____	13. I am courteous.
_____	_____	14. I take pride in my personal appearance.
_____	_____	15. I do high-quality work.
_____	_____	16. I do accurate and neat work.
_____	_____	17. I am friendly and cheerful.
_____	_____	18. I follow company rules and regulations.
_____	_____	19. I control my temper.
_____	_____	20. I am loyal to my employer.
_____	_____	21. I do my work correctly and complete it on time.
_____	_____	22. I appreciate privileges and do not abuse them.
_____	_____	23. I have a good attitude.
_____	_____	24. I make an effort to improve.
_____	_____	25. I accept responsibility for my work.
_____	_____	**Totals**

Describe steps you can take to improve your work habits.

_____

_____

_____

_____

_____

_____

Being a Team Player

Reinforcing Vocabulary

Activity A

Chapter 14

Name _____

Date _____ Period _____

Complete the following definitions by writing the missing term in the preceding blanks.

argumentative   constructive criticism   ridicule
brainstorming   gossip   rumor
compromise   grapevine   sarcasm
conflict   harassment   teamwork

___brainstorming___   1. The process of _____ involves listing everyone's ideas, no matter how ridiculous the ideas may seem, and then discussing and evaluating them.

___sarcasm___   2. The use of cutting remarks is _____.

___gossip___   3. When you _____, you tell personal information about another person.

___teamwork___   4. Two or more people working toward a common goal is known as _____.

___ridicule___   5. To _____ a person is to make fun of him or her.

___argumentative___   6. A person who disagrees with just about everything can be described as _____.

___constructive criticism___   7. Offering judgmental remarks about a person or his or her work is _____.

___rumor___   8. A bit of information that passes from one person to another without proof of accuracy is a _____.

___grapevine___   9. An informal and unofficial flow of information is called a _____.

___conflict___   10. A _____ is a hostile situation resulting from opposing views.

___harassment___   11. Doing or saying things that make people feel different or uncomfortable is _____.

___compromise___   12. Giving something up to resolve a conflict is _____.

Tips for Getting Along

Activity B   Name _____

Chapter 14   Date _____ Period _____

Interview three people who each work in a different occupation. Ask each person to give five important tips for getting along with coworkers. List their responses in the space provided. (Student response.)

Occupation of First Person: _____

First Person's Tips:

1. _____

2. _____

3. _____

4. _____

5. _____

Occupation of Second Person: _____

Second Person's Tips:

1. _____

2. _____

3. _____

4. _____

5. _____

Occupation of Third Person:_____

Third Person's Tips:

1. _____

2. _____

3. _____

4. _____

5. _____

Why might some of the tips from the three people be similar? _____

_____

Why might some of the tips you were given be different? _____

_____

Do you agree with the tips listed above? Explain. _____

_____

_____

Do you disagree with any of the tips listed? Explain._____

_____

_____

_____

Studying Work Attitudes

Activity C

Chapter 14

Name _____

Date _____ Period _____

Carefully read each situation described below and respond to each request.

1. Imagine it is your first day on a new job. Describe what you would do to make a good impression on your coworkers and supervisors. Keep your answer in mind as you complete this activity.

   Demonstrate the qualities of a hard worker, be punctual, be courteous, be able to work well with

   others, and enjoy the work.

   _____

   _____

   _____

   _____

2. Now consider David, a stock clerk in a large supermarket. David does only what he is told to do, no more and no less. Does David have a good attitude toward work? Explain.

   No. Someone who has a good attitude toward work shows enthusiasm, helps others often, and

   always tries to perform at a high level. By failing to do any more than he is told, David does not

   show any of these characteristics.

3. One day, one of David's coworkers knocked over a product display. Boxes were scattered all over the floor. At the time, David was working nearby. If you were David, what should you have done in this situation?

   Help the coworker pick up the boxes.

   _____

   _____

4. David ignored the scattered boxes and left his workstation to tell others what had happened. David made a big joke at his coworker's expense. If you were David's supervisor, what would you say to David?

   He should have helped the coworker instead of making jokes about him.

   _____

   _____

5. If you were the worker who knocked over the display, what would you have said to David?

   It would have been nice if David had helped instead of laughing. Sometime in the future,

   David might be the one who needs help.

   _____

6. Later the same day, David was stocking shelves. The product he was stocking belonged in another part of the store. A coworker trying to help David told him he was making a mistake. However, David insisted he was right and started an argument. Was it proper for David to argue with his coworker?

   No.

(Continued)

Name _____

7. What do you think David should have done?

    If David thought he was correct, he should have checked with his supervisor instead of starting

    a fight with a coworker.

    _____

8. Before David went home that night, he overheard part of a conversation between two coworkers and their supervisor. The next morning, David told everyone what he had heard. The entire supermarket was soon exchanging comments on the news involving the coworkers. Was David correct in discussing what he had overheard? Explain.

    No. It was not intended that David hear the conversation. Therefore, he should have kept whatever

    he heard to himself.

    _____

    _____

    _____

    _____

    _____

9. When David's supervisor found out what had happened, she called David into her office for a conference. What do you think was said to David?

    She probably asked David why he was listening to the conversation and told him to never again

    gossip in the store.

    _____

10. If you were one of David's coworkers, what advice would you give to David?

    He should start concentrating more on his work than on what is happening around him or he may

    not have a job.

    _____

11. If you were David's supervisor, what would you do to help David become a better employee? Explain.

    (Student response.)

    _____

    _____

    _____

    _____

Good Work Habits in Action

Activity D   Name _____

Chapter 14   Date _____   Period _____

In your own words, explain how having the work habits listed below can help you get along with your coworkers. Give a specific example of how you could put each work habit into action. (Sample responses.)

Work Habits	Effect on Coworkers	Work Habits in Action
1. Being open to new ideas	Can aid in team planning.	Conduct a brainstorming session so each person can contribute ideas.
2. Respecting coworkers	They will appreciate your respect of their knowledge and skills.	Be willing to learn from coworkers.
3. Seeing coworkers' positive qualities	They will see your positive qualities.	Make positive comments about coworkers.
4. Showing trust	They will show support for one another.	Don't question a coworker's advice.
5. Admitting errors	They will appreciate your honesty.	Admit it if you get an order wrong and don't blame it on someone else.
6. Accepting constructive criticism positively	They will know you are willing to learn a better way to do the job.	Accept the criticism with a smile and thank them.

(Continued)

Name _____

Work Habits	Effect on Coworkers	Work Habits in Action
7. Keeping a positive attitude	They will think positively toward you.	Even when you are having a bad day, try to smile.
8. Having a good sense of humor	It can help them through difficult situations.	A joke or a funny comment can lighten a tough situation.
9. Avoiding the poor use of humor	Others won't see you as a clown or a slacker.	Take your job seriously.
10. Avoiding arguments	It can avoid conflict.	Keep the group functioning as a team.
11. Avoiding rumors	It can build trust.	Do not pass rumors on to others.
12. Avoiding harassment	They will feel respect and dignity.	Keep negative feelings out of the workplace.
13. Avoiding comparisons	They will feel more comfortable working with you.	Everyone will feel valued.

Chapter 15
Keeping Safety First

Reinforcing Vocabulary

Activity A   Name _____

Chapter 15   Date _____ Period _____

Match the following terms with their correct definitions.

___J___	1. Insurance against work-related accidents.	A. disability
___F___	2. A liquid that can easily ignite and burn rapidly.	B. dismissal
___D___	3. Oxygen, fuel, and heat: the three items that must be present for a fire to take place.	C. evacuate
___H___	4. Describes a plug that has an electrical connection with the earth to prevent shock.	D. fire triangle
___I___	5. A national act that calls for safe and healthy working conditions; also the title of a government agency.	E. first aid
___C___	6. To empty or vacate a place in an organized manner for protection.	F. flammable liquid
___E___	7. Immediate, temporary treatment given in the event of an accident or sudden illness.	G. FLSA
___A___	8. A temporary or permanent physical or mental condition that prevents an employee from working.	H. grounded
___B___	9. Another term for being fired.	I. OSHA
___G___	10. An act that protects the educational opportunities of youth and prohibits their employment in jobs that could endanger their health and safety.	J. workers' compensation

Preventing Accidents

Activity B   Name _____

Chapter 15   Date _____ Period _____

Select six of the occupations listed below and write them in the chart. For each occupation selected, describe an accident that could occur. Then list what could be done to prevent the accident. (Sample responses.)

Chef	Firefighter	Pilot
Salesclerk	Plumber	Truck driver
Secretary	Electrician	Farmer
Nurse's aide	Florist	Bookkeeper
Gas station attendant	Mason	Painter
Police officer	Flight attendant	Baggage handler

Occupation	Possible Accident	Preventive Measure
1. Chef	cut from knife	Handle knives by the handle not the blade.
2. Police officer	being shot	Wear a protective vest.
3. Firefighter	burns	Wear flame-resistant clothing.
4. Mason	stone chip in eye	Wear protective eyewear.
5. Painter	fall	Use a sturdy ladder.
6. Baggage handler	back injury	Lift using leg muscles, not back muscles.

Understanding Safety Practices

Activity C
Chapter 15

Name _____

Date _____ Period _____

Answer the following questions about safety on the job using the information provided in the chapter.

1. What should you do if you are not sure how to perform any part of your job? Ask your supervisor for further instruction.

2. Why might someone who is showing off be a hazard in the workplace? _____
   Show-offs take unnecessary chances.

3. How can open desk or file drawers be a hazard in a workplace? People can bump into or trip over open desk or file drawers.

4. Why shouldn't electrical machines or connections be touched with wet hands? Water is a good conductor of electricity. An electrical shock could cause serious injury or even death.

5. Why should workers avoid leaning too far back in their chairs? If a worker leans too far back in a chair, the chair could slip from beneath him or her.

6. Why should worn electrical cords or plugs be replaced? Frayed cords and bad connectors can create sparks and cause fires.

7. Why should electrical connections not be unplugged by pulling the cord? Pulling the cord could damage the protective insulated coating and cause a shock or start a fire.

8. Why should electrical circuits not be overloaded with too many machines or appliances? _____
   Overloading can cause wires to heat and start a fire.

9. When working with machinery, why should clothes fit snugly? Loose clothing can get caught in moving machinery.

10. Explain what type of shoes should be worn on industrial or construction work sites. _____
    Hard-toed safety shoes should be worn on industrial or construction worksites to protect feet from falling tools and equipment.

11. What six things should a smart worker know about lifting properly? A smart worker should know how much, how often, how far, and how high he or she can lift. He or she should also know how much help he or she needs and what mechanical aids are available to help.

12. Why should safety goggles be worn when using electrical tools and equipment? _____
    Safety goggles should be worn to protect eyes from dust and flying objects.

13. How should an object be lifted from the floor? Keep arms and back straight, bend the knees, then lift using the leg muscles.

(Continued)

Name _____

14. What types of accidents can occur in cluttered and messy work areas? tripping, slipping, and being struck by falling objects

15. What safety devices should be used when mopping a floor? safety cones or "wet floor" caution signs

16. Why should metal ladders not be used near electrical equipment or high-voltage wires? Metal conducts electricity. Someone standing on or touching a metal ladder could be seriously injured or killed if electrical contact is made with the ladder.

17. How close to your work should you position a ladder? within an arm's length

18. What two hazards cause nearly half of all fires each year? careless smoking and faulty electrical wiring

19. Why should oily rags and paper never be stored in open containers? They can build up heat and ignite.

20. What is the correct way to use the telephone to report a fire? Dial the fire station or the operator. Give your name, the company's name and address, and the exact location of the fire within the building.

21. What may happen if workers fail to wash their hands before eating or smoking? They may transmit harmful substances into their bodies.

22. Why should you stop working if you become ill on the job? You will not be working at top performance. Also, illness may cause you to be careless, leading to injury of you or someone else.

23. What should you do if you become injured on the job? You should report the injury immediately and get first aid right away.

24. When giving first aid, why should you check to see that an injured person does not have anything in his or her mouth or throat? Food or gum could keep the injured person from breathing.

25. Why was the Occupational Safety and Health Act passed? The Occupational Safety and Health Act was passed to reduce hazards in the workplace.

26. Why must employers place the OSHA poster in the workplace? Employers must place the OSHA sign in the workplace so employees know their rights and responsibilities under the act.

27. What will workers' compensation cover if a worker is injured on the job? Workers' compensation will cover the cost of unlimited medical treatment, payment of lost wages, income benefits for death, income benefits for disability, and insurance against occupational diseases.

Chapter 16
Handling Changes in Job Status

Reinforcing Vocabulary

Activity A

Chapter 16

Name _____

Date _____ Period _____

Match the following terms with their correct definitions.

___E___	1. Payment one-and-one-half or two times the regular wage that is given for hours worked beyond the normal 40-hour workweek.	A. commission
___A___	2. A percentage of the dollar amount of sales made.	B. fired
___F___	3. A set amount of money that is earned for a full year of work.	C. laid off
___C___	4. Being dismissed from a job for a reason beyond a worker's control, such as a cutback on production.	D. letter of resignation
___D___	5. A letter written to inform an employer that an employee is quitting his or her job.	E. overtime pay
___G___	6. A set amount of money that is earned for every hour of work.	F. salary
___B___	7. Being dismissed from a job due to poor performance or the inability to get along with others.	G. wages

Starting Full-Time Work

Activity B   **Name** _____

Chapter 16   **Date** _____ **Period** _____

Interview someone you know who has recently changed from part-time to full-time work. Record his or her answers to the questions that follow. Share what you learn with the class. (Student response.)

1. What caused you to change from part-time to full-time work? _____

_____

_____

_____

2. What do you like most about working full-time? _____

_____

_____

_____

3. What challenged you most when you first began working full-time? _____

_____

_____

_____

4. What changes surprised you when you became a full-time worker? _____

_____

_____

_____

5. How did your lifestyle change when you began working full-time? _____

_____

_____

_____

6. Based on what you learned, what advice would you give to someone preparing to change from part-time work to full-time work? _____

_____

_____

_____

_____

Changing Jobs

Activity C

Chapter 16

Name _____

Date _____ Period _____

The statements listed below are possible advantages and disadvantages of changing jobs. Place an *A* before each advantage and a *D* before each disadvantage. Afterward, join a small group of your classmates and compare your answers with others in the group. (Student response.)

_____ 1. A new job is a chance for a new beginning.

_____ 2. A new job is a chance for growth and promotion.

_____ 3. You may have to move.

_____ 4. You may earn a higher salary.

_____ 5. You may have opportunities for retraining or advanced learning.

_____ 6. You may be labeled a job hopper.

_____ 7. You will have new experiences and face new challenges.

_____ 8. You may lose accumulated paid sick leave.

_____ 9. You may have to rebuild vacation time.

_____ 10. You may receive better fringe benefits.

_____ 11. You will be dealing with many unknowns.

_____ 12. You may be able to travel.

_____ 13. You will have the chance to build new friendships.

_____ 14. You may have to leave a job you like.

_____ 15. You may lose seniority rights.

_____ 16. You may not receive as many fringe benefits as in your present job.

_____ 17. You may spend less time commuting to work.

_____ 18. You may be the lowest-ranked person in the new job.

Leaving a Job

Activity D　　　　　　　　　　Name _____

Chapter 16　　　　　　　　　　Date _____ Period _____

Read the letter of resignation below, written by Joe Left, and answer the questions that follow. Then rewrite the letter.

---

49 Crooked Road
Alsip, IL 60658
November 15, 20xx

Mr. Bruce Kovacs
The Music Store
100 Harmony Road
Alsip, IL 60658

Dear Mr. Kovacs:

I will be leaving at the end of this week. I have a much better job with Stereo-Recorder Company. You should have given me that raise I asked for yesterday. This wasn't such a great job, and I'm not sorry to leave.

Sincerely,

Joe Left

---

1. Did Joe give notice of his resignation far enough in advance? How much notice is recommended?
   No. Joe should have given notice two weeks in advance.

2. Is it acceptable for Joe to tell his employer that he has a better position? Explain. _____
   Yes, but he should have phrased it in a more positive way.

3. Should Joe have made the statement about the raise he didn't get? Explain._____
   No. Reasons for leaving a job and comments about a present employer should be stated in
   positive terms in order to avoid alienating the employer.

4. Explain what is wrong with Joe's last statement. Joe should either make a positive statement about
   the job or say nothing at all. After a statement like that, Mr. Kovacs is not likely to give Joe a good
   reference.

On a separate sheet of paper, rewrite Joe's letter to convey his message in a more positive way.

Job Changes Through a Career

Activity E   Name _____

Chapter 16   Date _____ Period _____

Read the following case study about the various job changes experienced by one worker during his career. Answer the questions related to the case.

Case Study

After graduating from college, Allen got a job as a technical writer with a small company. Allen had been working for the company for about a year when it was purchased by a major corporation. When the new owners reorganized the business, Allen was laid off.

1. What positive action could Allen have taken after losing his job? _Allen should have tried to maintain_

   a positive attitude. He needed to take a look at himself and think about his personality traits,

   interests, aptitudes, abilities, values, and career goals. He needed to get any necessary retraining

   and then look for another job.

Allen began a new job search and found a job as a laboratory assistant in a large company. Allen enjoyed his job, but he wanted to do more. He wanted to be promoted into the research and development group.

2. How could Allen prepare for the promotion he wanted? _Allen could attend classes to qualify him for_

   the position. He could find a mentor to advise him and work with him to develop the skills he needs.

   _____

   _____

Allen got his promotion and started working as part of a team to develop new product ideas. However, after four years, Allen is starting to think about changing jobs.

3. Why might Allen be thinking about changing jobs? _Allen might want a more challenging job._

   Perhaps he does not work well with his team.

   _____

   _____

4. What are some questions Allen should ask himself before making a decision to change jobs? _____

   What are my real reasons for leaving this job? Am I leaving to accept something better? Am I

   getting along with my boss and my fellow employees? Have I given myself and the job a chance?

   _____

5. Once Allen decides for sure that he wants to change jobs, what should he do? _Allen should start_

   looking for a new job before quitting his current job. When he is ready to quit, he should do so in a

   professional manner.

   _____

Report on Changes

Activity F   Name _____

Chapter 16   Date _____ Period _____

Read an article in a current magazine on one of the following topics:

- how to prepare for promotions
- what to do when you lose a job
- why people change jobs
- what other reasons cause changes in job status

Prepare a written report on the article and an oral report for the class. Be prepared to answer questions about the article. (Student response.)

Article title: _____

Author: _____

Source: _____

Report: _____

_____

_____

_____

_____

_____

_____

_____

_____

_____

_____

_____

_____

_____

_____

_____

_____

_____

_____

_____

_____

_____

Chapter 17
Basic Skills for Job Success

Reinforcing Vocabulary

Activity A

Chapter 17

Name _____

Date _____ Period _____

Match the following terms with their correct definitions.

__B__	1. Metric unit of weight that is less than one ounce.	A. degrees Celsius
__G__	2. To read something and mark any errors found in it.	B. gram
__H__	3. The group of words you know and use.	C. illiterate
__D__	4. Metric unit that measures volume and is slightly more than a quart.	D. liter
__C__	5. Word that describes a person who does not know how to read or write.	E. meter
__F__	6. A decimal system of weights and measures that is used by many countries.	F. metric system
__E__	7. Metric unit that measures distance and is slightly longer than one yard.	G. proofread
__A__	8. Metric unit for measuring temperature that is a little more than two degrees Fahrenheit.	H. vocabulary

Strengthening Your Vocabulary

Activity B   Name _____

Chapter 17   Date _____ Period _____

Read the following article on "Nutrition Facts." List any words in the article that are unfamiliar to you in the spaces that follow. Find these words in a dictionary and write their definitions.

Nutrition Facts

Dietitians have determined that limiting your intake of fats can help reduce your risk of atherosclerosis. They recommend that no more than 30 percent of your daily caloric intake come from fats. The average adult woman needs about 2000 Calories each day. This means that no more than 600 of those Calories should come from fat. The average adult man needs about 2700 Calories each day. A man, therefore, should limit his daily fat intake to 810 Calories.

Nutrition labels on food can help you analyze how much fat you are eating. Nutrition labels list the number of grams of fat in a serving of food. Each gram of fat equals nine Calories. Therefore, using the recommendations above, the average woman should eat no more than 67 grams of fat per day. The average man should eat no more than 90 grams of fat.

What kinds of foods are high in fats? Whole milk dairy products, choice grade meats, and desserts are some of the biggest culprits. One cup of whole milk contains eight grams of fat. A three-ounce piece of chuck roast may contain 26 grams of fat. A piece of cheesecake has about 18 grams of fat.

Don't let these figures make you too apprehensive. You can always fill up on fruits and vegetables! Foods like apples, oranges, carrots, and peas contain only traces of fat, and they are full of vitamins, minerals, and fiber.

Words	Definitions
1. (Sample response.) atherosclerosis	fatty deposits and fibrosis of the inner layer of the arteries
2. (Sample response.) calories	an amount of food having an energy-producing value of one large calorie
3. (Sample response.) culprits	a person accused of or charged with a crime
4. (Sample response.) apprehensive	viewing the future with anxiety or alarm
5. (Sample response.) fiber	mostly indigestible material in food that stimulates the intestine

Proofreading for Accuracy

Activity C

Chapter 17

Name _____

Date _____ Period _____

Proofread the following sentences. Mark any grammar, spelling, or punctuation errors you find. Then rewrite the sentences correctly. The first sentence has been done for you.

Example: When the dog tracks mud into the house Mrs Carson gets angry.

When the dog tracks mud into the house, Mrs. Carson gets angry.

1. When a student does not do their homework, they are given a detention.

   When students do not do their homework, they are given detentions. Or: When a student does not

   do his or her homework, he or she is given a detention.

2. Running, swimming, and bicycles are good forms of exersize.

   Running, swimming, and riding bicycles are good forms of exercise.

3. "Stop! she yelled.

   "Stop!" she yelled.

4. A cat will clean itself by licking it's fir.

   A cat will clean itself by licking its fur.

5. Clarence and Jim knows about the surprise there teacher has for the class.

   Clarence and Jim know about the surprise their teacher has for the class.

6. The room was pink and and green.

   The room was pink and green.

7. He wont go no matter how many times you ask him.

   He won't go, no matter how many times you ask him.

8. The project was due Tuesday march 27.

   The project was due Tuesday, March 27.

9. Your going to the store after work, aren't you.

   You're going to the store after work, aren't you?

Math Practice

Activity D

Chapter 17

Name _____

Date _____ Period _____

Practice using your math skills by solving the following problems. Do not use a calculator.

1. 25
    73
    12
    +6
    ̄1̄1̄6̄

2. 39.5
    +6.2
    ̄4̄5̄.̄7̄

3. 1/3 + 1/7 = 10/21

4. 943
    −21
    ̄9̄2̄2̄

5. 9.03
    −.72
    ̄8̄.̄3̄1̄

6. 5/12 − 1/4 = 1/6

7. 886
    ×62
    54,932

8. 7.2
    ×5.9
    42.48

9. 1/3 × 1/2 = 1/6

10. 52)1144 (22)

11. .5)10.45 (20.9)

12. 3/8 ÷ 2 = 3/16

13. Write 0.66 as a percentage. 66%

14. Write 91% as a decimal. .91

15. Suppose you, as a cashier, are given a five dollar bill for a $3.52 purchase. What coins and bills should you return to the customer? 1 one-dollar bill, 1 quarter, 2 dimes, and 3 pennies

16. Suppose you, as a cashier, are given a $20 bill for a $16.71 purchase. What coins and bills should you return to the customer? 3 one-dollar bills, 1 quarter, and 4 pennies

17. Suppose you, as a cashier, are given a $20 bill and a $10 bill for a $22.43 purchase. What coins and bills should you return to the customer? 1 five-dollar bill, 2 one-dollar bills, 2 quarters, 1 nickel, and 2 pennies

18. Convert 6 inches to centimeters. 15.24 centimeters

19. Convert 52 kilograms to pounds. 114.4 pounds

20. Convert 13 gallons to liters. 49.27 liters

Time Management and Study Skills

Reinforcing Vocabulary

Activity A

Chapter 18

Name _____

Date _____ **Period** _____

Complete the following definitions by writing the missing term in the preceding blanks.

attitude   memory   tests
concentrate   priorities   time
IRS time   procrastination   time log
key   review   time management

concentrate   1. To focus your effort and attention on something is to _____.

time   2. Poor use of _____ is a common cause of poor study habits.

memory   3. Do not rely on your _____ to recall important things to do.

priorities   4. All the things you consider highly important are _____.

key   5. When taking notes, listen carefully and write down the _____ points.

procrastination   6. Delaying decisions or activities is _____.

tests   7. The purpose of _____ is to measure how much you know and don't know.

IRS time   8. _____ _____ is short for Individual Responsibility for Saving Time. It involves taking steps to make the best use of your time.

review   9. After you study, take time to mentally _____ the material.

time log   10. A written record of a person's use of time is a(n) _____ _____.

time management   11. Planning and carefully using time is called _____ _____.

attitude   12. A positive _____ will help you begin your study assignment.

Time Log

Activity B
Chapter 18

Name _____

Date _____ Period _____

Learn how you spend your time by keeping a time log for one week. Fill in the blocks in the chart below to indicate the amount of time you spend each day with each activity. Indicate time in hours to the nearest quarter-hour (15 minutes = .25 hour; 30 minutes = .50 hour; 45 minutes = .75 hour). Remember that the total time spent for all your combined activities should equal 24 hours each day. At the end of the week, total your time for each activity. (Time log is student response.)

	Sun	Mon	Tues	Wed	Thurs	Fri	Sat	Total Hours
Sleeping								
Eating								
Grooming								
Going to school								
Studying or doing homework								
Working at a job								
Doing household tasks								
Participating in extracurricular activities								
Watching TV or listening to music								
Phoning/messaging friends								
Visiting friends								
Reading and relaxing								
Doing other activities								
Total Number of Hours	24	24	24	24	24	24	24	168

Time Log Review

Activity C   **Name** _____

Chapter 18   **Date** _____ **Period** _____

Review the time log you completed in Activity B. Then answer the questions that follow as you refer to the time log. (Student response.)

1. What activity used the most time? _____

2. How many hours did you spend doing chores?

   A. Average hours per day: _____

   B. Total weekly hours: _____

3. How many hours did you spend doing homework and studying?

   A. Average hours per day: _____

   B. Total weekly hours: _____

4. How many hours did you spend taking part in extracurricular activities?

   A. Average hours per day: _____

   B. Total weekly hours: _____

5. How many hours did you spend working?

   A. Average hours per day: _____

   B. Total weekly hours: _____

6. How many hours did you spend watching TV, listening to music, and surfing the Internet?

   A. Average hours per day: _____

   B. Total weekly hours: _____

7. How many hours did you spend reading and relaxing?

   A. Average hours per day: _____

   B. Total weekly hours: _____

8. How many hours did you spend visiting friends?

   A. Average hours per day: _____

   B. Total weekly hours: _____

9. How many hours do you usually sleep per day? _____

10. About how much time do you spend eating each day? _____

11. About how much time do you spend grooming each day? _____

12. About how many hours per day do you spend talking on the phone? _____

13. About how much total weekly time do you spend doing other activities? _____

14. Are you spending your time on your most important priorities? _____

15. When do you usually do your homework and study? Is this the best time of day for you to study?

_____

(Continued)

Name _____

16. Do you usually spend more time doing homework and studying or working? _____

17. Do you spend enough time studying? _____

18. Do you spend enough time relaxing? _____

19. Do you spend enough time doing chores? _____

20. Which activities are taking up too much of your time? Can you reduce the time spent on these activities?

    _____

    _____

    _____

21. Are you usually able to complete important tasks on time? _____

22. Are you a good time manager now? _____

23. What daily habits would you like to change to improve the use of your time? _____

    _____

24. What new habits can you develop to give yourself more free time? _____

    _____

25. How could you use the free time gained? _____

    _____

26. What steps can you take to make your study time more effective? _____

    _____

    _____

    _____

IRS Time

Activity D　　　　　　　　　　Name _____

Chapter 18　　　　　　　　　　Date _____ Period _____

Place yourself on IRS Time by filling in the following "To Do" list with all the tasks you want to accomplish within the next week. Check the A column for tasks that you absolutely must do, the B column for tasks that you should do next, and the C column for tasks you will do if there is time. Follow your list for two days, checking off tasks as you complete them. Then answer the questions at the bottom of the page.

("To Do" list is student response.)

Priority

A	B	C	To Do	Completed
___	___	___	1. _____	_____
___	___	___	2. _____	_____
___	___	___	3. _____	_____
___	___	___	4. _____	_____
___	___	___	5. _____	_____
___	___	___	6. _____	_____
___	___	___	7. _____	_____
___	___	___	8. _____	_____
___	___	___	9. _____	_____
___	___	___	10. _____	_____
___	___	___	11. _____	_____
___	___	___	12. _____	_____
___	___	___	13. _____	_____
___	___	___	14. _____	_____
___	___	___	15. _____	_____
___	___	___	16. _____	_____
___	___	___	17. _____	_____
___	___	___	18. _____	_____
___	___	___	19. _____	_____
___	___	___	20. _____	_____

Do you think you have a responsibility to save time? Explain. (Answers may vary. Students' responses should reflect an understanding of the content on text pages 315–316.)

_____

_____

What steps could you take to manage your time better? (Sample response.) make a to-do list each day; organize your time according to priorities; avoid procrastination; reduce interruptions; focus on one task at a time

Good and Poor Study Habits

Activity E

Chapter 18

Name _____

Date _____ Period _____

Identify each of the following study habits as good or poor. Then in the appropriate column, indicate how often you practice each habit by writing always, sometimes, or never. (Frequency is student response.)

Good Habits	Poor Habits	Study Habits
always, sometimes, or never		1. Take notes in class.
always, sometimes, or never		2. Take notes when you read assignments.
	always, sometimes, or never	3. Study in a cluttered area.
always, sometimes, or never		4. Follow directions.
always, sometimes, or never		5. Gather all the supplies you need before you start to study.
	always, sometimes, or never	6. Study in an area where you will be distracted.
always, sometimes, or never		7. Set priorities for your time.
	always, sometimes, or never	8. Put off big assignments until the last day.
	always, sometimes, or never	9. Do all your studying the night before a test.
always, sometimes, or never		10. Work in an area that is quiet and relaxing.
	always, sometimes, or never	11. Study and review the easy parts first.
always, sometimes, or never		12. Do what must be done first.
	always, sometimes, or never	13. Study the tough parts last.
	always, sometimes, or never	14. Try to do two activities at the same time.
always, sometimes, or never		15. Study when you are rested.
always, sometimes, or never		16. Take a few moments after you study to think about what you studied.
	always, sometimes, or never	17. Study while watching TV.
always, sometimes, or never		18. Do a little each day on big assignments that are due in a week or more.

Chapter 19
Communication Skills

Reinforcing Vocabulary

Activity A

Chapter 19

Name _____

Date _____ Period _____

Complete the following definitions by writing the missing term in the preceding blanks.

active listening   communicate   nonverbal
aggressive   complimentary   passive
assertive   feedback   public
body language   multitasking   verbal

public   1. Making speeches before audiences is known as _____ speaking.

passive   2. A person with a(n) _____ communication style avoids conflict and usually has low self-esteem.

active listening   3. Listening and responding to improve mutual understanding is _____.

nonverbal   4. The sending and receiving of messages without the use of words is _____ communication.

body language   5. A form of nonverbal communication in which messages are sent through body movements, facial expressions, and hand gestures is _____ _____.

assertive   6. A person with a(n) _____ communication style respects others while honestly expressing opinions and attitudes.

feedback   7. The return of information to the sender in order to check the accuracy of the communication is _____.

verbal   8. The type of communication involving the use of words is _____ communication.

multitasking   9. Doing more than one job at a time is known as _____.

communicate   10. To share ideas, feelings, or information is to _____.

aggressive   11. A person with a(n) _____ communication style achieves goals at the expense of others.

complimentary   12. A phrase placed at the end of a letter, such as *sincerely* and *yours truly*, is a _____ close.

Speech Evaluation

Activity B

Chapter 19

Name _____

Date _____ Period _____

Using your own paper, write a two-minute speech on one of your favorite topics, such as a hobby, interest, or personal experience. Write notes for your speech on note cards and use them as you give your speech to the class. Then use the forms below to evaluate yourself and one classmate. Circle the numbers in the rating scale that best describe the speech presentations. Complete both forms and give the bottom one, unsigned, to your teacher.　(Evaluations are student response.)

Evaluating Yourself

Topic of speech:_____

	Poor	Fair	Good	Very Good	Excellent
Had well-organized information:	1	2	3	4	5
Appeared calm and confident:	1	2	3	4	5
Showed enthusiasm:	1	2	3	4	5
Used proper grammar:	1	2	3	4	5
Spoke clearly:	1	2	3	4	5
Used varied tone of voice:	1	2	3	4	5
Spoke at good volume:	1	2	3	4	5
Spoke at good speed:	1	2	3	4	5
Kept good eye contact:	1	2	3	4	5
Had good posture:	1	2	3	4	5
Positive remarks:	1	2	3	4	5
Areas to improve next time:	1	2	3	4	5

Evaluating a Classmate

Evaluation of (name):_____

Topic of speech:_____

	Poor	Fair	Good	Very Good	Excellent
Had well-organized information:	1	2	3	4	5
Appeared calm and confident:	1	2	3	4	5
Showed enthusiasm:	1	2	3	4	5
Used proper grammar:	1	2	3	4	5
Spoke clearly:	1	2	3	4	5
Used varied tone of voice:	1	2	3	4	5
Spoke at good volume:	1	2	3	4	5
Spoke at good speed:	1	2	3	4	5
Kept good eye contact:	1	2	3	4	5
Had good posture:	1	2	3	4	5

Positive remarks: _____

Areas to improve next time: _____

Telephone Practice

Activity C   Name _____

Chapter 19   Date _____ Period _____

Practice your telephone skills by completing the following exercises.

I. Receiving a Call

Imagine it is 12:10 p.m. on January 6 and you are in charge of answering the telephone at work. The caller, Bill Russell of Briswell Corporation, asks to speak with Maria Romero. Maria is on her lunch break. The caller wants to check an order he placed two weeks ago. His number is (609) 555-2232. Bill wants Maria to call him back. Use the form below to record this message.

To _Maria Romero_____

Time _12:10 p.m._____   Date _January 6_____

While You Were [OUT]

Mr._Bill Russell_____

of_Briswell Corporation_____

Phone #_(609) 555-2232_____

☐ Telephoned   ☒ Please call back
☐ Came to see you   ☐ Will call again
☒ Left the following message

_He wants to check on an order he placed two_____
_weeks ago._____
_____
_____

II. Placing an Order

Imagine you work for Baxter Ford and your boss has asked you to call Bob Jensen at A to Z Parts Warehouse, (201) 555-0010, to place an order. You want three chrome handles for a 2001 Ford (part number A-1562-C) and two rear-seat speaker grills in black plastic (part number A-1378-BF). Your work phone number is (201) 555-1292. Your work address is 5937 Kingston Drive, Northern Springs, IN 52392. Plan your call by answering the following questions.

1. What company do you represent? _Baxter Ford_____

2. Who are you calling? _Bob Jensen at A to Z Parts Warehouse_____

3. What telephone number are you calling? _(201) 555-0010_____

4. Why are you calling? _to order parts_____

5. What parts are you ordering? (Fill in the chart)

(Continued)

Name _____

Part Description	Part Number	Color	Quantity
1. Chrome handles	A-1562-C	Chrome	3
2. Rear seat speaker grills	A-1378-BF	Black	2

III. Making an Emergency Call

Imagine you work for Goodman Office Supplies, located at the corner of Brice and Bethel. One of the workers, Arnie Potter, just tripped over some boxes in the warehouse. He is lying on the floor, moaning in pain and holding his leg. Arnie is near retirement. He is in generally good health, but you know he suffers from high blood pressure. Role-play your telephone conversation for the class as you call for an ambulance.

Complete the following chart with the emergency phone numbers your family should have. Post a copy of this list near each phone in your home. (Numbers are student response.)

Emergency Phone Numbers

Fire _____

Ambulance _____

Gas Company _____

Police _____

Doctor _____

Electric Company _____

State Police _____

Poison Control Center _____

Water Company _____

Others:

_____   _____

_____   _____

_____   _____

_____   _____

Remember, if you do not know what number to call in an emergency, just dial the operator.

Writing Business Letters

Activity D   Name _____

Chapter 19   Date _____ Period _____

Imagine you work for Edwards & Frederickson Financial Services. Your offices are located at 144 Grand Avenue, Centerville, NJ 08701. Your boss has asked you to help gather information about a new computer system. You are to write to Mr. Alvin J. Grant, president of Grant's Computer Company, 11 Lee Avenue, Southtown, NJ 04532, to request information about the new model BRX-527 computer system. You also need information about types of software packages available and those most suited for your office. Write your letter in the space below following the business letter format illustrated in the text. (Sample response.)

Edwards & Frederickson Financial Services
144 Grand Avenue
Centerville, NJ 08701

Today's date, 20XX

Mr. Alvin J. Grant, President
Grant's Computer Company
11 Lee Avenue
Southtown, NJ 04532

Dear Mr. Grant:

My company, Edwards & Frederickson Financial Services, is planning to update our computer system. Please send me information about the new model BRX-527 computer system. I would also like to receive information regarding the software packages available and your recommendations for which types would best suit our office.

Thank you for your assistance.

Sincerely,

Student's signature

Student's name

Understanding Body Language

Activity E

Chapter 19

Name _____

Date _____ Period _____

Based on your first impression, write what you think each example of body language communicates. Then draw or describe three more examples of body language and tell what each communicates. Discuss your thoughts with others in class. (Sample responses are shown.)

1. joy, sorrow, pain

6. reservation, displeasure, disagreement, defiance

2. friendliness, humor, happiness, affection, approval, ridicule

7. greeting, shared secret, signal, teasing

3. a wish or hope, good luck, a lie

8. (Student response.)

4. greeting, farewell, agreement, peace, sportsmanship

9. (Student response.)

5. defiance, a threat, power

10. (Student response.)

Chapter 20
Your Appearance

Reinforcing Vocabulary

Activity A   Name _____

Chapter 20   Date _____ Period _____

Match the following terms with their correct definitions.

__D__	1. Items that are popular for only a short period of time.	A. accessories
__B__	2. A skin disorder caused by inflammation of the skin glands and hair follicles.	B. acne
		C. dress code
__E__	3. Cleaning and caring for your body and clothes.	D. fads
__A__	4. Items such as shoes, handbags, belts, neckties, and jewelry that are needed to complete outfits.	E. grooming
		F. wardrobe inventory
__C__	5. A set of rules that individuals must follow regarding clothing and general appearance.	
__F__	6. A list of all the clothes and accessories you have in your closet and drawers.	

In the space below, write a paragraph or two about someone who is getting ready for work. Correctly use all the chapter terms listed above.

(Sample response.) Jerome practices good *grooming* habits when getting ready for work. He bathes

daily and cares for his complexion to reduce *acne*. When he started working, Jerome took a *wardrobe*

inventory and identified the new clothes he needed. To make the most of his money, Jerome bought

classic clothes and avoided *fads* that will soon go out of style. When dressing for work, Jerome

chooses outfits that follow his company *dress code*. His *accessories* are minimal and professional.

_____

_____

_____

_____

_____

_____

_____

_____

Check Your Grooming Habits

Activity B | Name _____
Chapter 20 | Date _____ Period _____

Answer the following questions by placing a check in the column that best describes your grooming habits.
(Student response.)

	Always	Usually	Sometimes	Never
1. Do you keep your hair neat and clean?				
2. Do you shower or bathe daily?				
3. Do you use a deodorant or antiperspirant daily?				
4. Are your nails clean and well manicured?				
5. Do you brush and floss your teeth regularly?				
6. If you wear makeup, is it applied lightly for a natural look?				
7. If you wear fragrance, is it light and pleasant?				
8. Do you wear appropriate clothing to school?				
9. Do you wear appropriate clothing to work?				
10. If you wear jewelry, does it accent your clothing?				
11. Do your accessories coordinate with your clothing?				
12. Does your clothing fit properly?				
13. Do you wear clean clothing?				
14. Is your clothing free from wrinkles?				
15. Are your shoes clean or shined?				

What can you do to improve your grooming habits? _(Answers may vary. Students' responses should_
reflect an understanding of the content on text pages 350–352.)

_____

_____

What Workers Wear

Activity C

Chapter 20

Name _____

Date _____ Period _____

Make a list of all the clothing that you feel would be appropriate for each of the following workers.

Computer programmer:

(Sample response.) collared shirt and trousers,

blouse or sweater with slacks or a skirt

_____

_____

_____

_____

Construction worker:

(Sample response.) work pants and shirt, work

boots, hard hat, any other protective

clothing needed

_____

_____

_____

_____

Bank teller:

(Sample response.) business suit, collared shirt

and trousers, blouse or sweater with slacks or

a skirt

_____

_____

_____

_____

Insurance salesperson:

(Sample response.) business suit

_____

_____

_____

_____

_____

_____

Department store clerk:

(Sample response.) knitted shirt with a collar and

trousers, informal blouse or sweater with slacks

or a skirt

_____

_____

_____

Janitor:

(Sample response.) uniform, if required, or work

pants and shirt, work boots

_____

_____

_____

_____

List six occupations requiring a uniform. (Sample responses are shown.)

firefighter _____

flight attendant _____

food service worker _____

housekeeper _____

nurse _____

police officer _____

List six occupations for which your school clothes would be suitable.

(Student response.) _____

_____

_____

_____

_____

_____

Wardrobe Planning for Work

Activity D   Name _____

Chapter 20   Date _____ Period _____

You get the most from your clothing dollar when you carefully plan your wardrobe. Begin planning by listing the clothes you own that fit into each of the categories below. Then identify the job you would like to hold and make a complete list of the clothes you would need for it. Compare the clothes you need to what you already own. Then make a final list of clothing to buy for work.   (Student response.)

School Clothes	Casual Clothes	Dressy Clothes

The job I would like to have is:_____

Work Clothes I Need	Work Clothes I Must Buy

Chapter 21
Good Health and Job Success

Reinforcing Vocabulary

Activity A
Chapter 21

Name _____

Date _____ Period _____

Complete the following definitions by writing the missing term in the preceding blanks.

addiction
balanced diet
drug
drug abuse

drug screening
nutrients
physical fitness
stress

Answer	Definition
drug abuse	1. A term that describes the reckless use of drugs is _____ _____.
stress	2. A feeling of tension, strain, or pressure is _____.
nutrients	3. The chemical substances in foods that nourish the body are _____.
balanced diet	4. An intake of food that supplies all the needed nutrients in the amounts needed to maintain good health is called a(n) _____ _____.
drug	5. A(n) _____ is any chemical substance that brings about physical, emotional, or mental changes in people.
physical fitness	6. The ability to perform daily tasks easily with enough reserve energy to respond to unexpected demands is _____ _____.
addiction	7. The never-ending obsession to use a drug is called _____.
drug screening	8. A test that can reveal the presence of drugs in a person's body is a _____ _____.

In the space below, write a paragraph or two about someone who knows the importance of good health to job success. Correctly use all the chapter terms listed above.

(Sample response.) Dana understands the importance of good health. She eats a *balanced diet*, chooses foods that are high in fiber and *nutrients*, and makes *physical fitness* a priority. In addition, she manages *stress* well and maintains a positive work-life balance. Dana prevents *drug abuse* and *addiction* by avoiding *drugs*. As a result, she is not at risk of jeopardizing her employment in the event of a *drug screening*. Her healthy lifestyle leads to success and productivity at work.

A Balanced Diet

Activity B   Name _____

Chapter 21   Date _____ Period _____

Jeff was hoping that he could make the basketball team next year. In order to do so, he knew he needed to be in excellent physical condition. Jeff had put on a few extra pounds from eating too much fast food and drinking too many sodas. He had heard about the MyPyramid.gov Web site you could use to find out what you should eat each day. He logged on and selected *MyPyramid Plan*. He entered the information requested—his age, gender, and activity level—and his personalized plan was created. It included the following recommendations for each day's food intake based on a 2800-calorie pattern:

Grains: 10 ounces
Vegetables: 3 ½ cups
Fruits: 2 ½ cups
Milk: 3 cups
Meat & beans: 7 ounces

Plan a day's menus for Jeff based on these recommendations. Be sure to include the correct amounts from each group in your sample menus. Also follow the recommendations of the Dietary Guidelines for Americans summarized in Figure 21-1 in your text. (Menus are student response.)

Sample Daily Menus	
Breakfast	**Dinner**
Lunch	**Snacks**

Totals:

Grains:_____ Fruits:_____ Meat & beans:_____

Vegetables: _____ Milk:_____

Learning About Stress

Activity C   Name _____

Chapter 21   Date _____ Period _____

Answer the following questions about how you view stress. Then, share your thoughts with a small group
of classmates.   (Student response.)

1. Place a check in the blank in front of each activity or situation you consider stressful.

    _____   A. going swimming
    _____   B. going on your first date
    _____   C. having a job interview
    _____   D. taking your driver's test
    _____   E. giving a speech
    _____   F. moving to a different town
    _____   G. playing softball
    _____   H. going on a picnic
    _____   I. starting a new job
    _____   J. reading a book
    _____   K. placing an order by telephone
    _____   L. training a new person at work
    _____   M. taking a surprise quiz

2. List three more activities you consider stressful.

    A. _____

    B. _____

    C. _____

3. Place a check in the blank in front of each activity or situation that you feel helps reduce stress.

    _____   A. taking part in physical activities like jogging, bicycling, and swimming
    _____   B. having good eating and sleeping habits
    _____   C. drinking a lot of coffee and other drinks that contain caffeine
    _____   D. talking to someone about your problems
    _____   E. complaining about your problems
    _____   F. trying to get away from it all for a few minutes
    _____   G. planning the use of your time
    _____   H. being involved in civic or social groups
    _____   I. reading a book
    _____   J. playing a game
    _____   K. listening to music

4. List three of your own ideas for reducing stress.

    A. _____

    B. _____

    C. _____

Avoiding Substance Abuse at Work

Activity D   Name _____
Chapter 21   Date _____ Period _____

Imagine you are an employer. Answer the following questions related to tobacco, alcohol, and drug use in your company.

1. What would your employee handbook say regarding your policy on smoking? (Student response.)
   _____
   _____
   _____
   _____

2. What would be the advantages of having a smoke-free workplace? (Answers may vary.) increases
   the productivity and health of employees; protects employees from secondhand smoke; helps
   smokers cut back or quit
   _____
   _____

3. How would you help an employee who wanted to quit smoking? (Student response.)
   _____
   _____
   _____
   _____

4. What would your employee handbook say regarding your drug and alcohol policy? _____
   (Student response.)
   _____
   _____
   _____
   _____
   _____

5. What would be the advantages of having an alcohol- and drug-free workplace? (Answers may
   vary.) increases the productivity and health of employees; reduces absenteeism and lateness;
   reduces safety risks; promotes good relationships among coworkers; decreases the risk of
   internal theft
   _____

6. How would you help an employee who had an alcohol or drug problem? (Student response.)
   _____
   _____
   _____
   _____

Developing Leadership Skills

Reinforcing Vocabulary

Activity A

Name _____

Chapter 22

Date _____ Period _____

Match the following terms with their correct definitions.

___E___	1. A person who influences the actions of others.	A. agenda
___G___	2. The president, vice president, secretary, and treasurer of a student organization.	B. career goals
___J___	3. The most common reference used in parliamentary law.	C. career/technical student organization
___A___	4. A list of activities that will occur during a meeting.	D. committee
___H___	5. An orderly way of conducting a meeting and discussing group business.	E. leader
___I___	6. The person who usually conducts a group's meetings.	F. leadership
___C___	7. Groups that help students develop leadership skills and prepare to work in certain occupational areas.	G. officers
___F___	8. The ability to lead or direct others on a course or in a direction.	H. parliamentary procedure
___D___	9. A group within an organization that handles a specific function of the organization's work.	I. president
___B___	10. Something members of career/technical student organizations share.	J. Robert's Rules of Order

Being a Good Leader

Activity B   Name _____

Chapter 22   Date _____ Period _____

Describe how a leader could demonstrate each leadership trait listed. You may use examples from your own experiences or create new ones. (Sample responses are shown.)

1. A good leader respects other people. Example: _A member of a project team listens carefully and without interruption to other members' ideas, concerns, and opinions._

2. A good leader accepts responsibility and works within the group. Example: _A classmate who works on a group project researches his assigned topic and delivers a report to the group on time._

3. A good leader gets along with others in a friendly and peaceful manner. Example: _One of the members of the cheerleading squad is nice to everyone on the team and fosters positive relationships._

4. A good leader gives praise where praise is due. Example: _A teacher congratulates a student on improving her study skills and test scores._

5. A good leader communicates thoughts and feelings in a clear and understandable manner. Example: _A member of a service club communicates his choice for the club's annual project, supporting his opinions with logical reasons._

6. A good leader is well informed on matters that concern the group. Example: _One of the members of the debate team organizes the annual debate schedule and updates all members regularly with any changes._

7. A good leader is confident and honest. Example: _An employee admits to making a mistake on a recent project and shares what she learned in an effort to help the company avoid future challenges._

8. A good leader is positive and excited about the group's goals. Example: _The leader of the school dance committee enthusiastically supports the decoration committee's choice of theme and colors._

9. A good leader is open-minded and can help set group goals. Example: _The president of a career/technical student organization helps members develop a plan to raise funds for attending a national competition._

10. A good leader can get the group started and keep it on track. Example: _The captain of the basketball team organizes and leads team practices._

Learning About Career/Technical Student Organizations

Activity C

Chapter 22

Name _____

Date _____ Period _____

The chart below lists some of the larger state and national career/technical student organizations. Write a brief description of each organization and list the classes that you feel relate to each organization.

Organization	Description of Organization	Classes That Relate
1. Business Professionals of America (BPA)	helps students learn job-related skills for careers in business management, office administration, and information technology	(Student response.)
2. DECA—An Association of Marketing Students	for students who are interested in the broad business of marketing	(Student response.)
3. Family, Career, and Community Leaders of America (FCCLA)	for students who have taken or will take courses in family and consumer sciences	(Student response.)
4. Future Business Leaders of America—Phi Beta Lambda (FBLA-PBL)	helps students understand American business enterprise and set career goals for the business field	(Student response.)
5. Health Occupations Students of America (HOSA)	for students interested in health occupations	(Student response.)
6. National FFA Organization (FFA)	for students preparing to enter careers in agriculture, agribusiness, and agriscience	(Student response.)
7. SkillsUSA	offers training and employment opportunities for students preparing to enter the workforce	(Student response.)
8. Technology Student Association (TSA)	for students who are taking or have taken technology courses	(Student response.)

Which organizations described above interest you? Why?

_____(Student response.)_____

_____

_____

_____

Your Career-Related CTSO

Activity D   Name _____

Chapter 22   Date _____ Period _____

Research a career/technical student organization to which you belong or would like to join. Then answer the following questions.

1. What career/technical student organizations are in your school? <u>(Answers may vary.) Business</u>
   <u>Professionals of America (BPA); DECA—An Association of Marketing Students; Family, Career,</u>
   <u>and Community Leaders of America (FCCLA); Future Business Leaders of America (FBLA-PBL);</u>
   <u>Health Occupations Students of America (HOSA); National FFA Organization (FFA); SkillsUSA;</u>
   <u>Technology Student Association (TSA)</u>

2. Which career/technical student organization is best suited to your interests and needs? _____
   <u>(Sample response.) Family, Career, and Community Leaders of America (FCCLA)</u>

3. Write the motto of this organization. <u>(Sample response.) "The Ultimate Leadership Experience."</u>
   _____
   _____
   _____

4. What is the purpose of the organization? <u>(Sample response.) To promote personal growth and</u>
   <u>leadership development through Family and Consumer Sciences education.</u>
   _____
   _____

5. What are the colors of the organization? What does each of the colors mean? <u>(Sample response.)</u>
   <u>Red and white. Red symbolizes strength, courage, and determination—personal qualities leading</u>
   <u>to happiness through a positive self-image. White stands for sincerity of purpose and integrity of</u>
   <u>action, qualities that will help individuals build a better tomorrow.</u>

6. Describe the symbol of the organization. <u>(Sample response.) The symbol shows the name of the</u>
   <u>organization inside a large swooping arch. It also shows the organization's motto, "The Ultimate</u>
   <u>Leadership Experience."</u>
   _____

7. What are the parts of the symbol and what do they mean? <u>(Sample response.) The collegiate</u>
   <u>lettering represents the organization's focus on education and student leadership. The large</u>
   <u>swooping arch embodies an active organization that moves toward new arenas.</u>
   _____

8. Describe the official dress of the organization. <u>(Sample response.) Red blazer, collared shirt,</u>
   <u>necktie, dress shoes, dress socks or nylons.</u>
   _____
   _____

Paychecks and Taxes

Reinforcing Vocabulary

Activity A

Chapter 23

Name _____

Date _____ Period _____

Match the following terms with their correct definitions.

___I___   1. A length of time for which an employee's wages are calculated. Most businesses have weekly, biweekly, semimonthly, or monthly pay periods.

___E___   2. The total amount of money earned during a pay period.

___H___   3. The amount of money left after all deductions have been taken from the gross pay.

___D___   4. Employee's withholding allowance certificate; a form filled out by an employee when beginning a new job. It determines how much of the employee's pay should be withheld for taxes.

___A___   5. A person, such as a child or nonworking adult, who relies on a taxpayer for financial support.

___C___   6. Wage and tax statement; a form showing how much a worker was paid and how much income was withheld for taxes in a given year.

___G___   7. The agency that enforces federal tax laws and collects taxes.

___F___   8. A tax on all forms of earnings.

___B___   9. An act that allows the federal government to reserve a percentage of a paycheck for social security tax.

A. dependent
B. Federal Insurance Contributions Act (FICA)
C. Form W-2
D. Form W-4
E. gross pay
F. income tax
G. Internal Revenue Service (IRS)
H. net pay
I. pay period

Your Tax Dollars at Work

Activity C   Name _____

Chapter 23   Date _____ Period _____

Prepare a list of 10 questions for local and state government officials regarding how tax dollars are spent. Meet with the officials in person, write them a letter, or send questions via e-mail. Write your questions in the space provided. On the following page, write an article summarizing the answers to your questions.

Official(s) interviewed: (Student response.) _____

_____

Method(s) of contacting official(s): (Student response.) _____

_____

(Sample questions.)

1. What percentage of my tax dollar is used locally as opposed to overseas? _____

    _____

2. Who does social security help? _____

    _____

3. How many tax dollars go toward health care? _____

    _____

4. How many tax dollars go toward defense spending? _____

    _____

5. How many tax dollars go to fund federal disaster relief? _____

    _____

6. How does tax money help in conducting international affairs? _____

    _____

7. How does tax funding help in food and nutrition programs? _____

    _____

8. Does tax money go toward energy conservation? _____

    _____

9. Which countries benefit most from my tax dollars? _____

    _____

10. In your opinion, what is the biggest waste of tax dollars? _____

    _____

(Continued)

Name _____

Your Tax Dollars at Work

(Article is student response.)

_____

_____

_____

_____

_____

_____

_____

_____

_____

_____

_____

_____

_____

_____

_____

_____

_____

_____

_____

_____

_____

_____

_____

_____

_____

_____

_____

_____

_____

_____

_____

_____

_____

_____

Chapter 24
Budgets

Reinforcing Vocabulary

Activity A

Chapter 24

Name _____

Date _____ Period _____

Read each of the incomplete definitions below and decide which chapter term is being defined. Write the correct terms in the crossword puzzle.

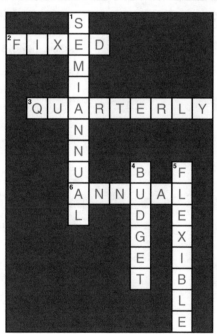

Across

2. A _____ expense involves a set amount of money due on a set date.
3. _____ expenses are paid four times a year.
6. _____ expenses are paid once a year.

Down

1. _____ expenses are paid twice a year.
4. A _____ is a plan for the use or management of money.
5. _____ expenses vary in amount.

Fixed and Flexible Expenses

Activity B   Name _____

Chapter 24   Date _____ Period _____

Read the list of expenses below and decide whether each expense listed is fixed or flexible. List each expense in the appropriate column of the chart.

Movie tickets	Telephone bills
Rent payments	Loan payments
Gasoline	Laundry
Jewelry	Books and magazines
New shoes	Ice cream
Mortgage payments	Auto insurance
Makeup	Automobile loan payments
Automobile maintenance	Birthday presents
Amusement park tickets	Savings

Fixed Expenses	Flexible Expenses
Rent payments	Movie tickets
Mortgage payments	Gasoline
Loan payments	Jewelry
Auto insurance	New shoes
Automobile loan payments	Makeup
	Automobile maintenance
	Amusement park tickets
	Telephone bills
	Laundry
	Books and magazines
	Ice cream
	Birthday presents
	Savings

Making Your Money Work for You

Activity C   **Name** _____

Chapter 24   **Date** _____ **Period** _____

Answer the following questions to help you evaluate your purchase goals before planning a budget.
(Student response.)

1. What are your current sources of income? _____

    _____

    _____

2. Identify three items you want to buy within a year and list them below in the *now* column. Also list
   three long-range purchases you want to buy in the *later* column. Use catalogs or newspaper ads to
   help you estimate the cost of the six items. Total each column.

	Now	Cost	Later	Cost
A.	_____	$_____	_____	$_____
B.	_____	$_____	_____	$_____
C.	_____	$_____	_____	$_____
	Total	$_____	Total	$_____

3. Will you be able to afford the items in your *now* column in a year or less? _____

    If yes, what is your next short-term purchase goal?_____

    _____

    _____

    If no, how could you increase your income?_____

    _____

    _____

4. Are you currently saving any of your income? _____

    If yes, what are your plans for the money you are saving? _____

    _____

    _____

    _____

    If no, how could you adjust your current spending pattern to start saving? _____

    _____

    _____

5. How can saving now help you reach some of your long-term purchase goals?_____

    _____

    _____

    _____

Planning a Budget

Activity D   Name _____

Chapter 24   Date _____ Period _____

Complete this form to develop a one-month budget for the lifestyle you desire. Include dollar amounts for the categories of spending that would apply to you.   (Student response.)

Monthly Budgeting Plan	
Estimated Income	**Estimated Flexible Expenses**
Net income (wages) _____	**Food**
Tips _____	At home _____
Other _____	Away from home _____
Total $ _____	**Clothing and Accessories**
	New clothes _____
Estimated Fixed Expenses	Cleaning and laundry _____
Housing	Accessories _____
Rent or mortgage payments _____	Grooming aids _____
Maintenance fees _____	**Household**
Monthly cable service _____	Home furnishings _____
Monthly Internet service _____	Maintenance and repair _____
Other _____	Gas _____
Insurance Premiums	Electricity _____
Life _____	Water _____
Health/medical _____	Telephone _____
Automobile _____	**Transportation**
Home _____	Gasoline _____
Other _____	Automobile maintenance _____
Debts and Obligations	Public transportation _____
Automobile loan payments _____	**Medical Needs**
Other installment loan payments _____	Doctor _____
Contributions _____	Dentist _____
Tuition _____	Other _____
Membership dues _____	**Savings**
Other _____	Savings account _____
Other _____	Investment/retirement account _____
Other _____	Other _____
Taxes and Licenses	**Recreation and Entertainment**
Property taxes _____	Movies _____
Automobile license plates _____	Vacations _____
Other _____	Sport events _____
Total $ _____	Books and magazines _____
	Other _____
	Total $ _____
Summary	
Total estimated income	$ _____
Total estimated expenses	
($ _____ fixed + $ _____ flexible)	– _____
Balance (income minus expenses)	$ _____

If you would have a positive balance (income greater than expenses), what would you do with the extra money? _____

If you would have a negative balance (income less than expenses), how would you adjust your income or expenses to have a workable budget? _____

Checking Accounts

Reinforcing Vocabulary

Activity A

Chapter 25

Name _____

Date _____ Period _____

Match the following terms with their correct definitions.

F	1. Is used to record how much money you put in your account.	A. bank statement
D	2. A written order to pay someone.	B. cashier's check
G	3. To sign your name on the back of a check made out to you so you can cash it.	C. certified check
I	4. To write checks for more money than you have.	D. check
A	5. A list of your deposits, withdrawals (in the form of checks), service charges, and interest payments.	E. debit card
		F. deposit slip
C	6. An item that guarantees payment; used by a bank to withdraw the requested amount from a checking account.	G. endorse
B	7. An item drawn by the bank on its own funds.	H. money order
H	8. An item that is an order to pay a certain amount of money to a certain party.	I. overdraw
J	9. Items purchased to avoid taking cash on vacation.	J. traveler's checks
E	10. Combines the functions of a check and an ATM card.	

Identifying Parts of a Check

Activity B	**Name** _____
Chapter 25	**Date** _____ **Period** _____

Examine the check below. On the next page, identify each of the numbered parts as indicated. Then give a brief description of each.

account number	check number	name and address
account open date	date	pay to the order of
amount in numbers	fractional routing number	routing number
amount in words	memo	signature

(Continued)

Check part:	Description:
1. name and address	identifies person(s) authorized to write checks on this account
2. account open date	the date the checking account was opened
3. pay to the order of	the party (person, company, organization) that is to receive the money
4. date	month, day, and year the check is written
5. check number	preprinted in sequence when checks are ordered
6. fractional routing number	a fractional version of the routing number
7. amount in numbers	must match the amount written in words
8. signature	should match the signature on your signature card
9. account number	checking account number
10. memo	what the check was written for
11. routing number	a 9-digit routing number specific to your bank
12. amount in words	the amount the check is written for

Using a Checking Account

Activity C

Chapter 25

Name _____

Date _____ Period _____

With the information below, practice writing checks, completing a deposit slip, and filling in a check register. The checks should be dated for October of the current year. Provide your name and address in the top left corners of the checks and the deposit slip. Your beginning balance is $150.10.

Check Number	Date	Transaction	
102	10/5	Shop Rite (groceries)	$50.00
103	10/11	Sears (charge account #23596)	$44.20
104	10/20	Easly Life Insurance Co.	$36.50
	10/21	Deposit (Check 16-214)	$250.00

(Continued)

Name _____

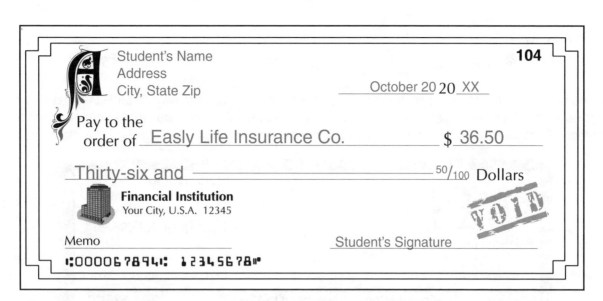

NUMBER	DATE	DESCRIPTION OF TRANSACTION	PAYMENT/DEBIT (–)	√ T	FEE (IF ANY) (–)	DEPOSIT/CREDIT (+)	BALANCE $ 150	10
102	10/5	Shop Rite	$ 50 00	$	$		50	00
		(groceries)					100	10
103	10/11	Sears	44 20				44	20
							55	90
104	10/20	Easly Life Insurance Co.	36 50				36	50
							19	40
	10/21	Deposit				250 00	250	00
							269	40

RECORD ALL CHARGES OR CREDITS THAT AFFECT YOUR ACCOUNT

REMEMBER TO RECORD AUTOMATIC PAYMENTS / DEPOSITS ON DATE AUTHORIZED.

Balancing a Checkbook

Activity D

Chapter 25

Name _____

Date _____ Period _____

Use the bank statement below and the check register on the next page to help Peter Banks balance his checking account. On the register, use the check (✓) column to check off items that appear on the bank statement. Complete the last form to make sure Peter's checkbook balances with his bank statement.

FI

Financial Institution

Statement for
Peter Banks
222 Atlantic Avenue
Toms River, NJ 58625

This statement covers
1/01/XX through 1/31/XX

Checking Account 123-4567		
Previous Statement Balance On 12/31/XX		525.10
Total of 2 **Deposits for**		2050.00+
Total of 4 **Withdrawals for**		410.00-
Total Interest Earned		0
Total Service Charges		10.00
New Balance		2155.10

Checks and Other Debits	**Check/Debit**	**Date Paid**	**Amount**
	ATM Withdrawl #00284	1/6	30.00
	Debit Card Withdrawl #33956 Foodsaver	1/17	95.00
	501	1/19	35.00
	Automatic transfer to account #09876543	1/30	250.00

Deposits and Other Credits		**Date Posted**	**Amount**
	Direct Deposit from #08549 on 1/11	1/11	1025.00
	Direct Deposit from #08549 on 1/25	1/25	1025.00

Thank you for banking with Your Financial Institution

(Continued)

Name _____

NUMBER OR CODE	DATE	DESCRIPTION OF TRANSACTION	PAYMENT/DEBIT (–)	√ T	FEE (IF ANY) (–)	DEPOSIT/CREDIT (+)	BALANCE
		AS–Automatic Deposit AP–Automatic Payment DC–Debit Card					$ 525 10
DC	1/6	Cash	$ 30 00	✓	$	$	30 00
							495 10
AD	1/11	Deposit		✓		1025 00	1025 00
							1520 10
501	1/16	T.J. Garage (Oil and lube)	35 00	✓			35 00
							1485 10
DC	1/17	Foodsaver (Groceries)	95 00	✓			95 00
							1390 10
AD	1/25	Deposit		✓		1025 00	1025 00
							2415 10
502	1/29	Pleasant Hill Apartment (February rent)	700 00				700 00
							1715 10
AP	1/30	Tranfer to Savings	250 00	✓			250 00
							1465 10
503	2/1	Medical Associates (Office visit co-pay)	30 00				30 00
							1435 10
504	2/3	Telephone Company (January phone bill)	41 75				41 75
							1393 35
	2/5	Deposit (birthday gift)				25 00	25 00
							1418 35
		Service Charge	10 00	✓			10 00
							1408 35

OUTSTANDING CHECKS

Check No.	Amount
502	700 00
503	30 00
504	41 75
TOTAL	771 75

Enter statement balance	2155 10
List deposits not credited on this statement and add to statement balance.	25 00
Subtotal	2180 10
Subtract checks outstanding	771 75
TOTAL	1408 35

Enter current checkbook balance	1418 35
Add any interest shown on statement	0
Subtract any charges shown on statement	10 00
New checkbook balance	1408 35

Correcting an Imbalance

Activity E   Name _____

Chapter 25   Date _____ Period _____

Karen's checkbook register does not balance with her bank statement. Check to make sure that Karen did not make any math errors in her register. Write the numbers that should appear in the balance column in the spaces provided beside the checkbook register. Then answer the following questions.

								BALANCE
		AS–Automatic Deposit	AP–Automatic Payment		DC–Debit Card			
NUMBER OR CODE	DATE	DESCRIPTION OF TRANSACTION	PAYMENT/DEBIT (–)	√ T	FEE (IF ANY) (–)	DEPOSIT/CREDIT (+)		$ 635 00
AP	2/3	Harrison's Motors (Car payment)	$ 235 00		$	$		235 00 / 400 00
207	2/7	Cindy Wright (Birthday present)	25 00					25 00 / 375 00
AD	2/7	Deposit				980 65		980 65 / 1355 65
208	2/9	City Utilities (January bill)	63 69					63 69 / 1293 66
209	2/11	ABC Wireless (Cell phone bill)	52 10					52 10 / 1241 56
DC	2/19	Exclusive Clothier (party dress)	152 68					152 68 / 1088 88
AD	2/21	Deposit				981 65		981 65 / 2070 53
211	2/25	Skyview Apartments (March rent)				695 00		695 00 / 1375 53

1. $400.00
2. $375.00
3. $1355.65
4. $1291.96
5. $1239.86
6. $1087.18
7. $2068.83
8. $1373.83

Checks and Other Debits	Check/Debit	Date Paid	Amount
	Automatic payment #04882 Harrison's Motors	2/3	235.00
	207	2/11	25.00
	ATM Withdrawl #77025	2/13	40.00
	Service Charge — ATM Withdrawl #77025	2/13	2.00
	208	2/14	63.69
	209	2/16	52.10
	Debit Card Withdrawl #79623 Exclusive Clothier	2/19	152.68
	210	2/23	59.70
	211	2/28	695.00
Deposits and Other Credits		Date Posted	Amount
	Direct Deposit from #09384 on 2/7	2/7	980.65
	Direct Deposit from #024731 on 2/21	2/21	981.65

9. Besides math errors, what other mistakes did Karen make? _She forgot to record a $40.00 ATM withdrawal, a $2.00 service charge, and check #210 for $59.70. She also recorded check #211 as a deposit/credit instead of a payment/debit._

10. What should the balance in Karen's register now read? _____
$1272.13 [$1373.83 – $40.00 – $2.00 – $59.70 = $1272.13]

Chapter 26
Savings

Reinforcing Vocabulary

Activity A

Chapter 26

Name _____

Date _____ Period _____

Complete the following definitions by writing the missing term in the preceding blanks.

annual percentage yield

annuity

certificates of deposit

compound interest

direct deposit

interest

money market account

mutual fund

principal

savings club

U.S. savings bonds

___mutual fund___ 1. A _____ _____ is a long-term investment that provides a way to invest in stocks and bonds.

___interest___ 2. Money paid to you for allowing a financial institution to use your money is known as _____.

___principal___ 3. The _____ is the amount of your original deposit in an account.

___compound interest___ 4. Interest that is earned on both the principal and the earned interest is _____ _____.

___savings club___ 5. An account into which you deposit a set amount of money every week or month is called a(n) _____ _____.

___certificates of deposit___ 6. _____ _____ _____ are purchased for a certain amount of money and are held for a set period of time.

___annual percentage yield___ 7 The _____ _____ _____ is the rate (or percent) of yearly earnings from an account.

___U.S. savings bonds___ 8. _____ _____ _____ are certificates of debt issued by the federal government.

___direct deposit___ 9. _____ _____ is a program that allows your employer to deposit your paycheck directly into your account.

___money market account___ 10. An account that is similar to a CD but has no time period restrictions is called a(n) _____ _____ _____.

___annuity___ 11. A(n) _____ is a form of investment that provides insurance as well as savings.

Financial Institutions

Activity B

Chapter 26

Name _____

Date _____ Period _____

Obtain brochures describing a commercial bank, savings bank, and credit union and the services they offer. Complete the chart with the information you learn about each. Then answer the questions below.
  (Chart is student response.)

Commercial Bank	Savings Bank	Credit Union
Name:	Name:	Name:
Location:	Location:	Location:
Hours:	Hours:	Hours:
Interest on savings accounts:	Interest on savings accounts:	Interest on savings accounts:
Interest on checking accounts:	Interest on checking accounts:	Interest on checking accounts:
Services offered:	Services offered:	Services offered:
Minimum balance required:	Minimum balance required:	Minimum balance required:
Fees:	Fees:	Fees:

In what ways are these financial institutions similar?   (Student response.) _____

_____

_____

_____

In what ways are these financial institutions different? (Student response.) _____

_____

_____

_____

If you were opening a new savings account, would you choose one of these institutions or an Internet bank? Explain. (Student response.) _____

_____

_____

_____

Savings Deposits and Withdrawals

Activity C

Chapter 26

Name _____

Date _____ Period _____

Use your name, today's date, and the information below to complete the deposit slip and withdrawal slip.

With the deposit slip, you want to receive a $50 bill after making the following deposit:

   bills—three twenties, one ten, and three singles

   coins—160 quarters, 100 dimes, 40 nickels, and 300 pennies

   checks—#14-610 for $32.10 and #70-7211 for $43.83

With your withdrawal slip, you want to withdraw $40 from your account.

SAVINGS DEPOSIT

Name Student's Name

Date Today's Date 20 ____

Financial Institution
Your City, U.S.A. 12345

CASH	CURRENCY	73	00
	COIN	55	00
CHECKS	14-610	32	10
	70-7211	43	83
TOTAL FROM OTHER SIDE			
TOTAL		203	93
LESS CASH RECEIVED		50	00
NET DEPOSIT		153	93

00-6789/0000

USE OTHER SIDE FOR ADDITIONAL LISTING

BE SURE EACH ITEM IS PROPERLY ENDORSED

⑆000067894⑆ 12345678⑈

ALL ITEMS ARE ACCEPTED SUBJECT TO OUR RULES AND REGULATIONS APPLICABLE TO THIS ACCOUNT

SAVINGS WITHDRAWAL

MUST BE PRESENTED BY THE SAVINGS CUSTOMER IN PERSON OR BY MAIL.

00-6789/0000

Name Student's Name

PLEASE TYPE OR PRINT CLEARLY

ACCOUNT NO. _____

Today's Date 20 ____

Forty and _____ 00/100 Dollars $ 40.00

DEDUCT ABOVE SUM FROM MY SAVINGS ACCOUNT ON DEPOSIT WITH:

Financial Institution
Your City, U.S.A. 12345

SIGN HERE Student's Signature

How Your Money Grows

Activity D

Chapter 26

Name _____

Date _____ Period _____

Use the chart below to answer the following questions about the power of compounding.

Year	\$10 Can Grow			
	Rate of Interest (compounded monthly)			
	5%	**7%**	**10%**	**12%**
1	\$123	\$125	\$127	\$128
2	253	258	267	272
3	389	402	421	435
4	532	555	592	618
5	683	720	781	825
6	841	897	989	1,058
7	1,008	1,086	1,220	1,320
8	1,182	1,289	1,474	1,615
9	1,366	1,507	1,755	1,948
10	1,559	1,741	2,066	2,323
15	2,684	3,188	4,179	5,046
20	4,128	5,240	7,657	9,991
25	5,980	8,148	13,379	18,976

How \$10 Can Grow

Note: The chart shows monthly contributions of \$10 with a return of 5%, 7%, 10%, and 12% compounded monthly for up to 25 years (figures have been rounded).

1. Determine how much your savings would be worth in 5 years if you contribute \$10 a month at the following interest rates:

    A. 5% __$683__

    B. 7% __$720__

    C. 10% __$781__

2. Why is it wise to compare interest rates before opening a savings account? _____

    The higher the interest rate, the more your savings will grow. _____

    _____

    _____

3. Assume you invest \$10 a month in an account with a 12% interest rate.

    A. What will your investment be worth in 25 years? __$18,976__

    B. How much money will you have contributed? __$3,000 [$10 × 12 months = $120 a year__
    __$120 × 25 years = $3,000]__

    C. How much of the account's value is due to interest? __$15,976 [$18,976 − $3,000 = $15,976]__

(Continued)

Name _____

4. How can compounding help you reach your long-term savings goals? With compounding, both your deposit and accumulated interest continue to earn interest and grow. Starting to save early and contributing regularly over a fixed period of time allows your money to benefit from the power of compounding.

5. If Henri saves $10 a month, earning 10% interest, how much will he have saved in six years? $989

6. Tia just celebrated her 25th birthday. If Tia saves $10 a month, earning 10% interest, how much will she have saved by age 50? $13,379

7. How much more savings will Tia have than Henri? $12,390 [$13,379 − $989 = $12,390]

8. T.J. would like to start saving for a cruise vacation. He estimates that he will need at least $1,000 for his trip.

   A. If he opens a savings account that earns a 7% rate of interest and saves $10 a month, how many years will it take to reach his goal? 7 years

   B. How could T.J. reach his goal more quickly? He could make larger monthly contributions or look for a savings account with a higher interest rate.

9. Brittany contributes $10 each month to her savings account. She currently has $1,755 in her account.

   A. Using the chart, determine the number of years that Brittany has been contributing to her account.
   9 years

   B. What is the interest rate on her account? 10%

10. Develop a savings plan for one of your long-term savings goals. Include the monthly contribution, interest rate, and number of years needed to reach your goal. (Student response.)

Savings Survey

Activity E   **Name** _____

Chapter 26   **Date** _____ **Period** _____

If you have a savings account, answer the following questions based on your savings experience. If you do not have a savings account, use these questions to interview someone who does. Compare your answers with others in class.   (Student response.)

1. Is saving money important to you? Explain. _____

   _____

   _____

2. Rank the following reasons for saving in order of their importance to you—from 1 (most important) to 7 (least important).

   ____ emergencies
   ____ future income reduction
   ____ travel and recreation
   ____ advanced education
   ____ major purchases, such as a car or home
   ____ retirement
   ____ overall financial security

3. Aside from the seven reasons listed above, what other reasons do you have for saving money? _____

   _____

4. What are the advantages to saving money in a financial institution instead of at home? _____

   _____

5. What type of savings account do you have? _____

6. In what type of financial institution is your savings account? _____

7. What interest rate does your savings account earn? _____

8. How often is interest paid on your savings? _____

9. How often do you make deposits into your savings? _____

10. How often do you withdraw money from your savings? _____

11. Do you have more than one savings account? If so, describe your other account(s) in terms of the information included in Questions 5 through 10. _____

    _____

    _____

    _____

12. Besides a savings account, what other financial services offered by your financial institution have you used? _____

    _____

13. What advice would you give to someone who is considering opening a savings account? _____

    _____

Reinforcing Vocabulary

Activity A

Chapter 27

Name _____

Date _____ Period _____

Read each of the definitions below and decide which chapter term is being defined. Write the correct terms in the crossword puzzle.

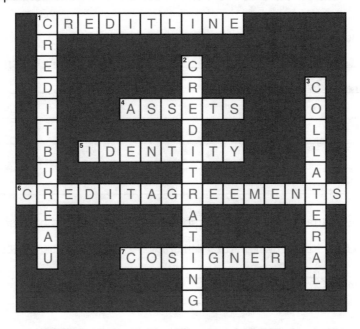

Across
1. The maximum amount a person can charge.
4. Valuable possessions you own, money you have in bank accounts, and the value of stocks and bonds you own are examples.
5. A type of theft that occurs when someone uses your personal information, such as your name, social security number, or credit card number without your permission to commit fraud or other crimes.
6. Contracts that legally bind a lender and a borrower to credit terms described in writing.
7. Someone who guarantees that your loan will be paid and must make the payments if you do not.

Down
1. Organizations that check credit applications and gather financial information on people to help businesses decide whether to grant or deny people credit.
2. An estimate of how likely you are to repay your bills on time.
3. Something of value held by a lending institution in case you fail to repay.

Credit Advantages and Disadvantages

Activity B   Name _____

Chapter 27   Date _____ Period _____

Read each statement. Write an *A* in the blank if the statement is an advantage of using credit. Write a *D* for each disadvantage of using credit. Then follow the directions below.

___A___   1. Credit is a convenience.
___D___   2. Credit encourages impulse buying.
___A___   3. Credit allows you to use goods and services while paying for them.
___A___   4. Credit helps you meet financial emergencies.
___D___   5. Credit ties up your future income.
___D___   6. Credit makes the costs of goods and services higher.
___D___   7. Credit can get you into serious debt.
___D___   8. Credit can cause you to overspend.
___A___   9. Credit allows you to shop and travel without the worry of carrying large amounts of cash.
___A___ 10. Credit spreads out the cost of expensive items over a period of time.

(Sample responses.)

Describe a real or fictitious situation in which a person uses credit wisely.

Chris wants to rent a car while on vacation. He uses a credit card to rent the car and then pays the

balance off before he incurs a finance charge.

_____

_____

_____

_____

Describe a real or fictitious situation in which a person abuses credit and is harmed by the misuse.

Jane uses her credit card to buy everything, from small purchases to large ones. At the end of the

month she is surprised at the amount of the bill and can only pay the minimum amount. She incurs

finance charges month after month.

_____

_____

For what types of items would you use credit?

vacations

large appliances and electronics for which the purchase has been planned

_____

For what types of items would you avoid using credit?

impulse items

routine items

_____

The Cost of Credit

Activity C Name _____

Chapter 27 Date _____ Period _____

Complete the following exercises to figure the cost of using various types of credit.

Credit Cards

Your credit card balance for this month is $60. You can pay the full balance or make a minimum payment of $10 each month. If you choose to make the minimum payment, you will be charged 1.5 percent interest per month (18 percent annual interest) on the unpaid balance. The steps below show how to figure the cost of carrying an unpaid balance.

Step 1: Subtract the minimum payment from the total balance to get the remaining balance.

$60.00 − 10.00 = $50.00

Step 2: Multiply the remaining balance by the interest rate (.015). This is the cost of delaying full payment for another month.

$50.00 × .015 = $ 0.75

Step 3: Add the answers to steps one and two to find the new balance that will appear on next month's bill. Use this figure to begin the calculations for next month (Month 2).

$50.00 + .75 = $50.75

Figure the total cost of making minimum payments until the bill is paid off by repeating the above steps.

Month 2:
Step 1: $50.75 − 10.00 = $ 40.75
Step 2: $ 40.75 × .015 = $ .61
Step 3: $ 40.75 + .61 = $ 41.36

Month 3:
Step 1: $ 41.36 − 10.00 = $ 31.36
Step 2: $ 31.36 × .015 = $ .47
Step 3: $ 31.36 + .47 = $ 31.83

Month 4:
Step 1: $ 31.83 − 10.00 = $ 21.83
Step 2: $ 21.83 × .015 = $ .33
Step 3: $ 21.83 + .33 = $ 22.16

Month 5:
Step 1: $ 22.16 − 10.00 = $ 12.16
Step 2: $ 12.16 × .015 = $ .18
Step 3: $ 12.16 + .18 = $ 12.34

Month 6:
Pay remaining balance in full at this time. $ 12.34

Add together the six monthly payments. $ 62.34

Then subtract the original total balance from this sum. What was the total cost of delaying full payment on this credit card bill? $ 2.34

Installment Credit

The cash price of a television is $600.00. However, you can purchase it on credit by paying $100.00 cash now and $46.67 monthly for one year.

Step 1: Multiply the amount of each payment by the number of payments.

$ 46.67 × 12 = $ 560.04

Step 2: Add the cash payment to the answer in step 1. This is the total cost of the television.

$ 560.04 + 100.00 = $ 660.04

Step 3: Subtract the cash price from the answer to step 2. This is the cost of using credit.

$ 660.04 − 600.00 = $ 60.04

The Credit Game

Activity D

Chapter 27

Name _____

Date _____ Period _____

Evaluate your credit history as you play the game below with two or three of your classmates. Use buttons or circles of paper for markers. Take turns flipping a coin to move around the board. If the coin is flipped "heads," move the marker two spaces. If the coin is flipped "tails," move the marker one space. The player who finishes first is the winner. (Game is student response.)

1. Start	2. Your savings account shows a steady pattern of saving over the last three years. Move ahead 1 space.	3.	4. Your charge accounts with the local gas and electric companies show that you frequently pay late fees. Move back 1 space.
8.	7. You are already spending 20 percent of your take-home pay on installment debts. You cannot afford any more credit. Go back to start.	6. Someone has stolen your credit card and other identity information and has made fraudulent purchases. Miss one turn to get the matter resolved.	5. You just got a job! Your steady source of income makes you a good credit risk. Take another turn.
9. You pay the total due on your gasoline credit card on time each month. Move ahead 2 spaces.	18. Easy credit has caused you to fall into a pattern of impulse buying. Miss a turn to give yourself time to plan your next purchases.	17.	16. You have a reputation for making payments on time at a local department store. Move ahead 1 space.
10. Your credit cards are always charged to the limit and you've carried a large unpaid balance for the last 15 months. Miss a turn while you pay off some of your debt.	19.	20. Congratulations! You've shown that you can manage money responsibly and use credit wisely.	15. Your loan fell through because the credit bureau said that your cosigner has a worse credit history than you do. Move back to space #10.
11.	12. You purchased a new TV on installment credit. You failed to make your payments and the set was repossessed. Move back 1 space.	13. You've repaid a loan to your company credit union in a timely fashion. Take another turn.	14.

Chapter 28
Insurance

Reinforcing Vocabulary

Activity A

Chapter 28

Name _____

Date _____ Period _____

Match the following terms with their correct definitions. Then write a paragraph using the chapter terms to describe a fictitious person's insurance situation.

__D__	1. A managed health care plan insurance for which members pay a set fee and receive medical care, as needed, from a participating doctor or hospital.	A. deductible
__H__	2. A managed health care plan in which an organization of doctors or hospitals contract with an insurance company to provide health services.	B. disability insurance
__F__	3. Insurance designed to provide financial security to the family of the insured, if that person dies.	C. dividend
__G__	4. A legal contract describing the rights and responsibilities of a person purchasing insurance and those of the company offering it.	D. health maintenance organization (HMO)
__I__	5. The amount of money paid for insurance.	E. insurance claim
__A__	6. The amount a policyholder must pay before an insurance company will pay a claim.	F. life insurance
__E__	7. Requesting payment from your insurance company for a covered loss.	G. policy
__C__	8. A payout, usually annual, on money earned on whole life insurance.	H. preferred provider organization (PPO)
__B__	9. Insurance that provides for people who become unable to work due to serious illness or injury. It allows disabled employees to receive a percentage of their incomes for an extended period of time.	I. premium
__J__	10. Insurance that protects your possessions against fire, theft, or other types of loss. Property insurance also provides liability coverage in the event that someone is injured in your home.	J. property insurance

(Sample response.) Kelly visited her insurance agent to discuss insurance. She wants to find out about *property insurance* to protect her home. She is also comparing *health maintenance organizations (HMOs)* and *preferred provider organizations (PPOs)* for medical coverage. She is looking for a *policy* that has a low *premium* as well as a low *deductible*. Her agent also tells her how *disability insurance* and *life insurance*, which can pay a *dividend*, can protect her and her family's finances. The agent also explains how to file a *claim* if she has a loss.

Car Insurance Costs

Activity B   **Name** _____

Chapter 28   **Date** _____ **Period** _____

Contact a local insurance company. Request the necessary information to complete the form below regarding automobile insurance coverage. Then choose the types of coverage you would like to have and figure your total premium. Compare your form with classmates to see if another company would offer you lower rates. (Student response.)

Company _____

1. What are the premium costs for the following types of coverage?

   A. Bodily injury insurance _____

   What is the limit of liability per person?_____ per accident? _____

   B. Property damage insurance _____

   What is the limit of liability per accident? _____

   C. Collision insurance _____

What deductibles are available?_____

2. What other types of auto coverage are available and what is the cost for each type?

   A. _____

   B. _____

   C. _____

3. What discounts are available and what is the value of each?

   A. _____

   B. _____

   C. _____

List the types of automobile coverage you would buy and the cost for each type.

	Coverage	**Cost**
A.	_____	_____
B.	_____	_____
C.	_____	_____
D.	_____	_____
E.	_____	_____
		Total _____

List the discounts for which you would qualify and the value of each discount.

	Discount	**Value**
A.	_____	_____
B.	_____	_____
		Total _____

Subtract the total value of the discounts from the total cost of the insurance. What is your total premium?

_____

Personal Property Inventory

Activity C

Chapter 28

Name _____

Date _____ Period _____

Keeping a current record of your property will help you in reporting lost or stolen property. Use this form to take inventory of your property.   (Student response.)

Item Description (Include brand name, model #, and/or serial # when possible.)	Date of Purchase	Purchase Price and Tax	Place of Purchase

Understanding Insurance

Activity D   Name _____

Chapter 28   Date _____ Period _____

Answer the following questions to show your understanding of the concepts presented in the chapter.

1. What is the difference between the insurer and the insured? _The insurer is the insurance company,_
   while the insured is the person who purchases the insurance.
   _____

2. What type of automobile insurance protects you against the claims of other people?_____
   liability insurance

3. What type of automobile insurance protects you against court actions or claims for injuries to other people?
   bodily injury insurance

4. What type of automobile insurance protects other people's property against damage that you cause?
   property damage insurance

5. What type of automobile insurance pays for repairs to your car even if you are at fault? _____
   collision insurance

6. Why might a person decide not to carry collision insurance on his or her automobile?_____
   If a car is several years old, it might not be worth the cost of premiums and the deductible.

7. Name three costs besides hospital stays and examinations by physicians that may be covered under
   health insurance. _prescription drugs, eyeglasses, dental work_
   _____

8. What is an advantage of having group health insurance rather than buying health insurance on your own?
   group health insurance usually costs less

9. What is a *beneficiary*? _the person who is paid the face value of the policy if the insured dies_

10. What is *cash value*? _the amount of money you would receive if you cashed in the policy_

11. What is an advantage of term life insurance over whole life insurance? _The premiums for term life_
    insurance are less than the premiums for whole life insurance.

12. Compared with a married person, does a single person need more or less life insurance? _less_
    _____

13. Who receives benefits under disability insurance? _people who become unable to work due to_
    serious illness or injury

14. What is the purpose of property insurance? _to protect your possessions against fire, theft, or other_
    types of loss; to provide liability coverage in the event that someone is injured in your home

15. What type of property insurance pays the full cost of new items? _replacement value coverage_

16. How can a personal property inventory be helpful to a renter or homeowner? _It can help you decide_
    how much insurance to buy. It also provides a record of your valuables that would help you file a
    claim in the event of theft or fire.

17. Give an example of a situation in which you would need to file a claim. _(Student response.)_
    _____

Chapter 29
A Place to Live

Reinforcing Vocabulary

Activity A

Chapter 29

Name _____

Date _____ Period _____

Complete the following definitions by writing the missing term(s) in the preceding blanks.

furnished apartment
lease
real estate
rental agency

roommate
security deposit
unfurnished apartment
verbal agreement

unfurnished apartment   1. Store clearances and garage sales are good places to shop for low-cost items needed in a(n) _____ _____.

security deposit   2. An apartment owner will use a tenant's _____ _____ to make necessary repairs due to damage caused by the tenant.

lease   3. A(n) _____ explains in writing the rights and responsibilities of the tenant and the owner.

roommate   4. Living with a(n) _____ is an alternative to living at home or living alone.

rental agency   5. A(n) _____ _____ will refer a person to available apartments for a fee.

furnished apartment   6. A tenant who rents a(n) _____ _____ does not need to supply any of his or her own furniture.

verbal agreement   7. When a tenant and an owner agree on a rental arrangement without putting anything in writing, they make a(n) _____ _____.

real estate   8. Although most _____ _____ agencies handle the buying and selling of houses, some also handle rental properties.

Apartment Search

Activity B

Chapter 29

Name _____

Date _____ Period _____

Using the classified section of the newspaper or the Internet, gather information about one furnished and two unfurnished apartments to complete the chart below. Then answer the questions that follow.
(Student response.)

	Furnished Apartment	**Unfurnished Apartment A**	**Unfurnished Apartment B**
Address			
Number of bedrooms			
Monthly rent			
Utilities included in the rent			
Security deposit required			
Length of lease			
Amount of storage space			
On-site parking			
Nearby public transportation			
On-site laundry facilities			

Which of the three apartments you investigated would you most like to rent? Explain.

_____

_____

Which of the three apartments you investigated would you least like to rent? Explain.

_____

_____

Would you rather rent a furnished or an unfurnished apartment? Explain.

_____

_____

Would you rather live alone or share an apartment with a roommate? Explain.

_____

Furnishing an Apartment

Activity C

Chapter 29

Name _____

Date _____ Period _____

In the chart below, list all the furnishings you would need if you moved into an unfurnished apartment. Don't forget to include linens, dishes, cookware, cleaning supplies, and other household items. For each item listed, check the appropriate column to indicate whether you would borrow it or receive it as a gift, buy it used, or buy it new. Use the classified ads in your newspaper to estimate prices of the used items you plan to buy. Use store ads, catalogs, or the Internet to estimate prices of the new items you plan to buy. Then add the total of your planned purchases.   (Student response.)

Item	Borrow/ Gift	Buy Used	Buy New	Estimated Price
Total:				

Housing Costs

Activity D   **Name** _____

Chapter 29   **Date** _____ **Period** _____

Complete this activity to help you estimate the cost of moving into an apartment. (Student response.)

1. Assume you will rent one of the unfurnished apartments you investigated in Activity B. What is your monthly rent? _____

2. For all utilities not included in the rent, estimate their typical monthly bills. Ask the owner of the apartment or your local utility companies for estimates. Record all expenses that would apply to you.

   Electric company monthly bill   _____

   Gas company monthly bill   _____

   Water company monthly bill   _____

   Telephone company monthly bill   _____

   Total: _____

3. Add the totals from items 1 and 2.

   _____ + _____ = _____

4. Some guidelines suggest limiting your rent and utility costs to one-third of your take-home pay. Using this guideline, what would your take-home pay need to be if you were living in this apartment?

   _____

5. Some additional expenses occur when you first move into an apartment. Contact the apartment owner and your local utility companies to enter all expenses that would apply to you.

   Credit check by apartment owner   _____

   Security deposit for apartment   _____

   Electric company deposit   _____

   Gas company deposit   _____

   Water company deposit   _____

   Telephone company deposit   _____

   Furnishings (from Activity C)   _____

   Total: _____

6. List other items you would need to pay for if you were living in an apartment (food, laundry, transportation or gasoline, insurance, etc.). _____

   _____

   _____

7. After having completed the above, what have you determined about the cost of independent living?

   _____

   _____

8. What could you do to reduce some of your expenses? _____

   _____

   _____

Chapter 30
Transportation

Reinforcing Vocabulary

Activity A

Name _____

Chapter 30

Date _____ **Period** _____

Match the following terms with their correct definitions. In the space below, write a brief story about someone traveling to work. Correctly use all the terms in the story.

___D___ 1. A list of the expected arrival and departure times and locations for buses, trains, subways, and airplanes.

___A___ 2. A group of people who take turns driving to a common location or area.

___C___ 3. Transportation, such as buses or trains, used routinely by the general public.

___E___ 4. To change from one bus or train route to another in order to get to the right place.

___B___ 5. An organization that operates a transportation system.

A. car pool
B. carrier
C. mass transportation
D. schedule
E. transfer

___(Sample response for story.) Julia was offered a job downtown. As she considered the job offer, she___

___also considered how she would get to work. First, she considered *mass transportation*. She contacted___

___a *carrier* who provided her with a *schedule* and various options. When she reviewed the bus schedule,___

___she noted that she would have to *transfer* at two stops to get to her employer's office. She also noted___

___that the train station was several blocks from the office. However, the walk would not be bad during___

___good weather. Julia decided to take the train to work. Once she became acquainted with employees at___

___the office, she discovered that several of them lived near her. They have now decided to create a *car*___

___*pool*, which will save them all time and money.___

_____

_____

_____

_____

_____

_____

_____

_____

Reading a Bus Schedule

Activity B   **Name** _____

Chapter 30   **Date** _____ **Period** _____

Use the bus schedule on the next page to answer the questions below.

1. What telephone number would you use to find out what time you could catch a bus at the Broad Street stop? _555-TRIP_

2. What telephone number would you use to complain about a rude bus driver? _555-HELP_

3. On what holidays does this schedule operate? _Presidents' Day, Columbus Day, and Veterans Day_

4. On what days of the week does this schedule not operate? _Saturdays and Sundays_

5. What five activities are prohibited on the bus? _eating, drinking, smoking, littering, and loud radio playing_

6. Can passengers expect to get change from the bus driver? Explain. _No, passengers must have exact fare._

7. Approximately how many minutes is the ride from Green Street to Spring Road? _10 minutes_

8. On what bus line is the Park Avenue stop? _North Loop Line_

9. What does the O symbol mean? _transfer stop_

10. Suppose you arrive at Industry Park at 5:50 P.M. on the Downtown Express. How long will you have to wait at the stop for a North Loop bus to arrive? _5 minutes_

11. Which bus lines stop at Capitol Towers? _North Loop Line and Downtown Express_

12. What time does the first Downtown Express bus arrive at Industry Park? _7:50 A.M._

13. What time does the last bus of the day arrive at Glenwood Plaza, and which bus line is it? _____
    8:25 P.M., Center/Arbor Line

14. How would you get from Carson Parkway to Glenwood Plaza? _Take the North Loop Line and transfer at either Industry Park or Capitol Towers to the Downtown Express._

15. Suppose you live near the Center Street stop and have an appointment on Oak Street at 9:30 A.M. Which buses on which lines would you use to get there? _Pick up the Center/Arbor Line at the Center Street stop at approximately 8:40 A.M. Get off at Glenwood Plaza at 8:55 A.M. Transfer to the Downtown Express, taking the 9:15 bus. Arrive at Oak Street at approximately 9:25 A.M._

16. Name all the stops on the Center/Arbor line. _Center Street, Fountain Square, North Avenue, Glenwood Plaza, Cherry Drive, Orchard Lane, Arbor Trail_

RAPID BUS WEEKDAY RUSH	North Loop Line originates Columbus Blvd. 7:20 A.M.	Downtown Express originates Highland Rd. 7:45 A.M.	Center/Arbor Line originates Center St. 7:30 A.M.
Industry Park	7:55 A.M. 8:25 A.M. 8:55 A.M. 4:55 P.M. 5:25 P.M. 5:55 P.M.	7:50 A.M. 8:20 A.M. 8:50 A.M. 4:50 P.M. 5:20 P.M. 5:50 P.M.	——— ——— ——— ——— ——— ———
Fountain Square	7:35 A.M. 8:05 A.M. 8:35 A.M. 4:35 P.M. 5:05 P.M. 5:35 P.M.	——— ——— ——— ——— ——— ———	7:45 A.M. 8:45 A.M. 9:45 A.M. 6:15 P.M. 7:15 P.M. 8:15 P.M.
Capitol Towers	7:40 A.M. 8:10 A.M. 8:40 A.M. 4:40 P.M. 5:10 P.M. 5:40 P.M.	8:10 A.M. 8:40 A.M. 9:10 A.M. 5:10 P.M. 5:40 P.M. 6:10 P.M.	——— ——— ——— ——— ——— ———
Glenwood Plaza	——— ——— ——— ——— ——— ———	8:15 A.M. 8:45 A.M. 9:15 A.M. 5:15 P.M. 5:45 P.M. 6:15 P.M.	7:55 A.M. 8:55 A.M. 9:55 A.M. 6:25 P.M. 7:25 P.M. 8:25 P.M.

This schedule operates Monday through Friday, including Presidents' Day, Columbus Day, and Veterans' Day.

This schedule does not operate Saturdays, Sundays, or the following holidays: New Year's Day, Memorial Day, Independence Day, Labor Day, Thanksgiving, and Christmas.

For schedule information, call 555-TRIP.
For customer service, call 555-HELP.

Passengers must have exact fare. No eating, drinking, smoking, littering, or loud radio playing allowed on RAPID buses.

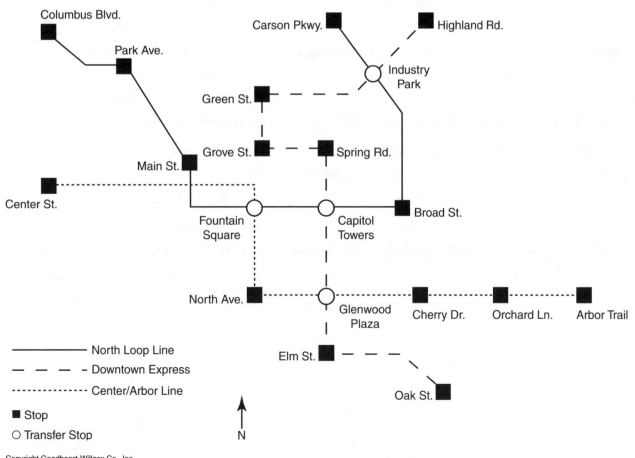

North Loop Line
Downtown Express
Center/Arbor Line

■ Stop
○ Transfer Stop

N

Transportation Comparison

Activity C   Name _____

Chapter 30   Date _____ Period _____

Complete the chart to express your view of the advantages and disadvantages of various types of transportation. Then answer the questions that follow.   (Sample responses.)

	Advantages	**Disadvantages**
Self-powered transportation Walking	good exercise	bad weather conditions
Riding a bicycle	inexpensive	unsafe in traffic
Automobile transportation Drive yourself	freedom to set own schedule	parking is expensive
Car pool	companionship	must accommodate everyone's schedule
Mass transportation Buses	inexpensive	transfers
Trains and subways	reliable	crowded
Airplanes	fast for long distances	expensive

1. Which type of transportation would you most likely use to get to work? Explain._____
   (Student response.) _____

2. Under what circumstances might you choose another type of transportation? _____
   (Student response.) _____
   _____

3. Which type of transportation would you least likely use to get to work? Explain._____
   (Student response.) _____
   _____

Chapter 31
Being a Responsible Citizen

Reinforcing Vocabulary

Activity A

Name _____

Chapter 31

Date _____ **Period** _____

Match the following terms with their correct definitions. Then write a paragraph using the chapter terms to describe what it means to be a responsible citizen.

E	1. The exclusive possession and control of a product or service.	A. bill
D	2. Two or more parties acting independently to offer the most favorable product or terms.	B. citizen
G	3. The right to complain and receive an appropriate response.	C. civil laws
B	4. A person who owes allegiance to a government.	D. competition
H	5. To submit one's name to the official list of citizens eligible to vote in elections.	E. monopoly
A	6. A proposed law.	F. public laws
C	7. Laws that define a person's rights in relation to other people.	G. recourse
F	8. Laws that define a person's rights in relation to government.	H. register

(Sample response.) To be a responsible *citizen* means to take an active role in government. One way you can do this is by taking the time to *register* to vote in elections. By voting, you elect officials who propose *bills*, which sometimes become laws. These laws include *civil laws* that define your rights in relation to other people and *public laws* that define your rights in relation to government. As you participate in the marketplace, you also have responsibilities as a citizen. Through *competition*, which gives you several choices, a *monopoly* can be avoided. However, when you make a choice and it does not meet expectations, you have the right to seek *recourse* and have the situation resolved.

_____

_____

_____

_____

_____

_____

_____

Voters' Survey

Activity B

Chapter 31

Name _____

Date _____ Period _____

Survey five adults about their voting habits and opinions. Record their responses in the chart provided. Compile your results with those of your classmates. Write an article for your school or local newspaper reporting your findings. (Student response.)

1. What is your sex?

2. What is your age?   A. 18 to 25   B. 26 to 40   C. 41 to 65   D. over 65

3. Are you registered to vote? (*Yes* or *No*)

4. How often do you vote?

    A. in most national, state, and local elections
    B. only in national elections
    C. never

5. How important is it for citizens to exercise their right to vote?

    A. very important
    B. somewhat important
    C. somewhat unimportant
    D. not important

6. What do you think is the most common reason some citizens do not vote?

    A. They are not familiar with the candidates and/or issues.
    B. They do not care about the results of the election.
    C. They do not feel their individual votes make a difference.
    D. They are too busy.
    E. (Write other reasons in the chart.)

7. Do you know the names of your elected officials? (*Yes* or *No*)

8. Do you feel you understand how laws are made? (*Yes* or *No*)

Survey Responses					
Question	Person 1	Person 2	Person 3	Person 4	Person 5
1.					
2.					
3.					
4.					
5.					
6.					
7.					
8.					

Classroom Council

Activity C   Name _____

Chapter 31   Date _____ Period _____

Hold a classroom election to elect seven students to serve as members of a classroom council—the governing body of your classroom. Complete the items below to pass a law in your classroom.

1. Write a law that you would like to propose to the citizens of your classroom. Be sure to choose the wording of your bill carefully. Citizens may not vote for bills that are not clear and specific.

    Students must volunteer two hours each week of free time to help a charity selected by the class.

    _____

2. List your reasons for wanting the law.

    A. It would help the charity.

    B. Students would feel good about themselves.

    C. It would provide a good experience for students.

3. You must be prepared to defend your bill against arguments by citizens who do not support it. List two reasons you think some may oppose the bill and provide a response to each.

    A. Reason: Students might not support the charity selected by the class.

    _____

    Response: If the majority of the class agrees to help a certain charity, then that is the one the

    class will help.

    B. Reason: Students should be able to determine how they spend their free time.

    _____

    Response: Volunteering is a good use of free time.

    _____

4. If you are not an elected council member, temporarily replace one of the students who is. Now that you have written your bill and prepared for the debate, present it to the class. Give citizens in your class time to debate the bill. List any new points that are mentioned during the debate.

    A. Points in favor: Students will make good use of their free time.

    Students will feel a sense of unity helping one charity.

    B. Arguments against: Students might not do a good job for a charity they do not support.

    The charity wants volunteers who believe in its cause.

5. Revise the wording of your bill based on comments made during the debate.

    Students must volunteer to help a charity of his or her choice for two hours each week.

    _____

6. Present your revised bill to the class. After completing any further discussion, have the council vote on your bill. What were the results of the vote? (Both numbers are student response.)

    (number) _____ votes for the bill

    (number) _____ votes against the bill

7. Based on this experience, what would you do differently if you were proposing this bill again?

    (Student response.)

    _____

Legal Advice

Activity D   **Name** _____

Chapter 31   **Date** _____ **Period** _____

Invite a lawyer, law student, or legal aide to class or interview one. Find out the answers to the questions below. (Student response.)

1. What are the most common reasons people seek the advice of a lawyer? _____
   _____

2. What is the best way to find a lawyer? _____

3. Are there any drawbacks to finding a lawyer through the Yellow Pages? _____
   _____

4. How useful is a state legal association in helping someone find a lawyer? _____
   _____

5. In what types of legal services do you specialize? _____
   _____

6. How important is it to choose a lawyer who is qualified to deal with a particular type of legal problem? Why is it important? _____
   _____

7. On the average, how much do legal services cost? _____

8. Where can someone who is unable to afford a lawyer get legal help? _____

9. How adequate are free legal services provided by a public service agency? _____
   _____

10. What problems could arise if a person fails to consult a lawyer in each of the following situations?

    A. when buying a house _____
       _____

    B. when getting a divorce _____
       _____

    C. when breaking a lease _____
       _____

    D. after receiving a summons or subpoena _____
       _____

    E. after being arrested _____
       _____

    F. when preparing a will _____
       _____

    G. when settling an estate _____
       _____

    H. when trying to resolve a consumer problem _____
       _____

Writing a Complaint Letter

Activity E

Chapter 31

Name _____

Date _____ Period _____

Write a complaint letter about one of the following consumer problems. Create any missing details. Be sure to use proper business letter format as shown in the text.

Problem #1:   You bought a tube of Brite White toothpaste. The label on the toothpaste claimed that your teeth would be noticeably whiter after using the toothpaste for just one week. You've been using the toothpaste for 10 days and you still haven't noticed a difference.

Problem #2:   You bought Old Favorites Jean Softener, a kit designed to give new blue jeans an old, faded look. You followed the directions on the package exactly. When you removed your jeans from the solution, they fell apart at the seams.

Problem #3:   You bought a Plushy Puppy stuffed toy for your nephew's birthday. While wrapping it, one of the eyes fell off. You noticed that the eye had a sharp point on it. You are concerned that your nephew could have been injured if he had been playing with the toy.

(Sample response.)

Student's name

8450 Anderson Avenue

Springfield, NJ 08701

Today's date, 20XX

Mr. Michael Stephens, President

Brite White, Inc.

412 Greenlawn Avenue

Ellis, NJ 04532

Dear Mr. Stephens:

I recently bought a tube of Brite White toothpaste. The label on the toothpaste claims that my teeth would be noticeably whiter after using the toothpaste for just one week. I have been using the toothpaste for 10 days and still haven't noticed a difference.

To solve my problem, I ask that you refund my money. Please find a copy of my purchase receipt enclosed.

I hope to hear from you soon. You may contact me at the above address or by phone at 732-555-8604.

Thank you for your assistance.

Sincerely,

Student's signature

Student's name

Citizen Awareness

Activity F   Name _____

Chapter 31   Date _____ Period _____

Read the following statements about topics from the chapter. Circle *T* if the statement is true or *F* if the statement is false.

T **(F)** 1. Any citizen of the United States who is at least 21 years old has the right to vote.

T **(F)** 2. Citizens are responsible for making laws.

(T) F 3. In order to vote, a citizen must register.

T **(F)** 4. Citizens can register to vote at most lawyers' offices.

(T) F 5. Federal laws are made by the United States Congress.

(T) F 6. A debate is the discussion of a proposed law by members of the legislature.

(T) F 7. Citizens may vote to accept a proposition, causing it to become a law.

(T) F 8. Local bills may be printed in the newspaper before being brought to a vote at town council meetings.

T **(F)** 9. The laws in the United States are divided into two categories—criminal laws and international laws.

(T) F 10. Civil laws relate to cases involving such issues as contracts, inheritances, and the business of corporations.

(T) F 11. Presidents, governors, and mayors are members of the executive branches of federal, state, and local governments, respectively.

T **(F)** 12. Most lawyers handle all types of cases, so any lawyer could deal with any legal problems a person might have.

T **(F)** 13. A person who is unable to afford a lawyer has no way to receive help with a legal problem.

T **(F)** 14. The only time a person needs a lawyer is if he or she is arrested.

(T) F 15. In a free enterprise system, both citizens and businesses have rights and responsibilities.

T **(F)** 16. Manufacturers can legally make any claims they wish on the labels of their products, whether or not they are true.

(T) F 17. Monopolies are against the law.

(T) F 18. Consumers have a responsibility to report products they find to be unsafe.

T **(F)** 19. Writing letters to the Better Business Bureau is the first step in correcting consumer problems.

(T) F 20. Generally, the BBB and a government agency will not handle the same complaint at the same time.